ZIPPO®

Advertising Lighters:

Cars & Trucks

Philip K. Taggart

Schiffer® Publishing Ltd

4880 Lower Valley Road, Atglen, PA 19310 USA

Dedication

This book is humbly dedicated
To my precious friend
Kristina Lynn Harris,
the "gentle whip that spurred the stubborn ass."

Library of Congress Card Number: 00-102075

Book Design by Anne Davidsen
Type set in Van Dijk/ Zurich

ISBN: 0-7643-1175-1

Printed in China
1 2 3 4

Published by Schiffer Publishing Ltd.
4880 Lower Valley Road
Atglen, PA 19310
Phone: (610) 593-1777; Fax: (610) 593-2002
E-mail: Schifferbk@aol.com
Please visit our web site catalog at
www.schifferbooks.com

We are always looking for people to write books on new and related subjects. If you have an idea for a book please contact us at the above address.

This book may be purchased from the publisher.
Include $3.95 for shipping.
You may write for a free catalog.

In Europe, Schiffer books are distributed by
Bushwood Books
6 Marksbury Ave.
Kew Gardens
Surrey TW9 4JF England
Phone: 44 (0)208 392-8585
Fax: 44 (0)208 392-9876
E-mail: Bushwd@aol.com
Free postage in the UK. Europe: air mail at cost

Please try your bookstore first.

Contents

*She passed the fan test

Acknowledgments

A book is almost never the work of a single person. In writing this little bit of "words in a row," I am extremely grateful to have met kind, knowledgeable, and helpful people as I prepared the text. Richard Weinstein, Mike Meuhlberger, Tony Zamisch, Michael Gover, Rickie Lee Spence, and Kenneth Nickolai sent me valuable lighters to be photographed and returned. Their trust and kindness are deeply appreciated.

Tucker Club founder Mark Boone provided much of the information included in the Tucker section. He also put me in touch with George Boucher and Raymond Parmenter, who provided me with photos of their original Tucker Zippo Lighters. Ed Pinedo and his wife Ann sent pictures of their lighter collection, as did Wally Laird. Ron Goudreau sent pictures of his Plymouth Roadrunner lighter, and Ken Poynter made available his rare Hudson lighters.

The Nash, Willys, and Tucker clubs were very helpful. Several members, including Rick Kamen and Jim Dworschack, provided photos of rare vehicles, as well as much enthusiastic encouragement.

During my two trips to Zippo Manufacturing, I was, almost literally, treated like family by those I met. Pat Grandy and Linda Meabon were exceptionally encouraging about this project. In addition to giving me access to the archives, they provided me with much of the new information that is in this book. Pat shares my love of cars, and time spent talking about cars and lighters will not be forgotten. Harry Schreiber, Art Director, and his assistant, Rita Walters, also provided much information regarding art application processes.

Linda Meabon, with Zippo Manufacturing since 1967, merits special mention. Currently the Zippo Archivist, she is a veritable font of knowledge regarding the history of Zippo Manufacturing and its lighters. She literally let me interrupt her daily work non-stop for several days, with highly detailed and time-consuming questions. She took time to mail me letters, return calls, write and answer e-mails, and encourage me when the mountain of information seemed too sheer to climb. She is an absolute treasure, and I offer her my humble thanks.

All these people have my thanks for the contributions they made to my book. Without each of them, this task would have been much more difficult.

Without Kristina Lynn Harris, however, this book would not have happened at all. She gave me the original idea, accompanied me to Bradford, and photographed many of the lighters in the book. (The good pictures are by her; most of the others are by me.) She helped photocopy the cardboards and edited almost every single word of the text, several times; but, most importantly, she provided me encouragement, support, and kind words when I needed them, which was often. She now knows far more about Zippo Lighters than she ever expected to. I am more grateful for her than words can say.

As interest in Zippo Lighters continues to grow, there is no doubt that new information will come to light. Everything contained here is as accurate as possible, given what we know about Zippo lighters today. Any mistakes, however, are wholly mine, and corrections are welcome.

Philip Kramer Taggart
Plano Texas
12-21-99

Introduction

In 1990, I played at the wedding of a friend who was a member of my infantry unit. As a thank-you gift, he gave me a polished chrome full-size Zippo lighter. This Zippo lighter, my first, is a cherished possession. I carried it for the rest of my Army career, before retiring it to my keepsake box in much the same way my father retired his own Army Zippo lighter—one that was a gift to him from his men during the Korean War.

As a child, I loved the feel of my Papa's Zippo lighter in my hands—a solid feel of something that said "quality." That sense of quality drove my father, and countless thousands of other soldiers, to save their Zippo lighters or pass them on to children as keepsakes. Soldiers simply did not discard their Zippo lighters.

Zippo lighters have always had a fascination for me. That fascination goes beyond the mere fact that Zippo lighters represent the absolute best the business world has to offer in terms of quality of product and service. I could never fully describe that fascination, any more than any collector in any field adequately could. Suffice it to say that it goes far beyond the utility of the product, encompassing everything from nostalgia to a desire to be part of something unique.

Such terms at least partially explain the typical old car lover as well. There isn't *really* any reason to own an old car. Modern vehicles are universally better in every way; they are better balanced, go faster, stop better, ride smoother, and are safer, quieter and more efficient. How then can one explain the envy I felt, driving a rented car to an "old car night" in Blasdell, New York, recently? I saw old cars—slow, heavy, huge—grossly inefficient in every way, and yet I wanted every one of them. The Willys 77, the 1958 Packard, the AMC Concord with 17,000 original miles, and the massive '48 Buick—I love them all, and I felt regret and envy as I got back into my state-of-the-art rented car to continue on my way. No collector can truly explain this yearning.

Ultimately, *why* people love and collect old cars and Zippo lighters is less important than the fact that they *do*. Disparate though they are, since 1935, the tiny tapestry of the Zippo lighter case has been intertwined with the automobile. The result is a marvelous story of flint and steel.

That story is worth telling.

PAPA'S ZIPPO

How heavy they seemed
in tiny hands, those
two inches by two ounces.
Brass centaur on the front,
bow taut, wary, ready
to protect vast shores
or little me.

On the back,
letters etched
as on a monument:

To
1LT George W Taggart
from his grateful men...

The rest of the inscription
is forgotten,
discarded—
to make room for other memories—
pre-dream dramas,
for Dearly Beloveds, of
Stories, Just So,
or Mongeese
that rikki-tick-ticked—and

And the memory of how heavy
those two ounces felt
in my tiny hands.

Philip Taggart

Zippo History

Zippo Lighter Origins

It is a good thing that there were no business consultants in 1932. If George Blaisdell had asked such a consultant for advice about introducing a high-priced luxury item like a cigarette lighter, at a price that equaled a large portion of the average worker's pay, the reply would have been simple. A surprised look from the consultant; some gentle words about the chances of success being "slim and none." The consultant might then have explained that simple cigarette lighters could be purchased for about 25 cents. Yes, they are crude, clunky, and require two hands. They usually work reasonably well, however, and anyway, "times are bad right now. Who can afford almost two dollars for a fancy match?" Then he would perhaps have escorted Mr. Blaisdell to the exit and gone about his business, shaking his head at such audacity.

Fortunately, George G. Blaisdell didn't make such a visit. When he completed the design of his new lighter (very loosely based on the two-handed Austrian lighter he was importing), he knew he had something special. The price would be high, but this was the "perfect match:" a one-handed flame that was impervious to wind. Many people would continue to buy the cheap 25-cent lighters, but there would also be those who both appreciated, and could afford, the quality and efficiency of his lighter. It is a tribute to the original design of the lighter that it has changed so little in the years since its inception. He called it "Zippo," a variation of the name "Zipper." *Interestingly, the actual name of the lighter was "Zippo" and not "The Zippo."*

Blaisdell added something to his lighter, a guarantee that became as famous as the lighter itself. The guarantee was that any Zippo lighter would be repaired or replaced for free, forever. Not just for the original owner, but for anyone, always.

As the years advanced from the dark days of 1932, the little lighter with the amazing guarantee became such an important part of American life that a Zippo lighter is now among the most collected pieces of 20th century Americana—a fitting tribute to George Blaisdell and his invention.

The first Zippo Manufacturing location.

THE FAMOUS

ZIPPO®

GUARANTEE

This rule or any Zippo rule, when returned to our factory, will be put in first-class mechanical condition free of charge, for we have yet to charge a cent for the repair of a Zippo rule regardless of age or condition. The finish, however, is not guaranteed.

ZIPPO MANUFACTURING CO., BRADFORD, PA.

The famous guarantee.

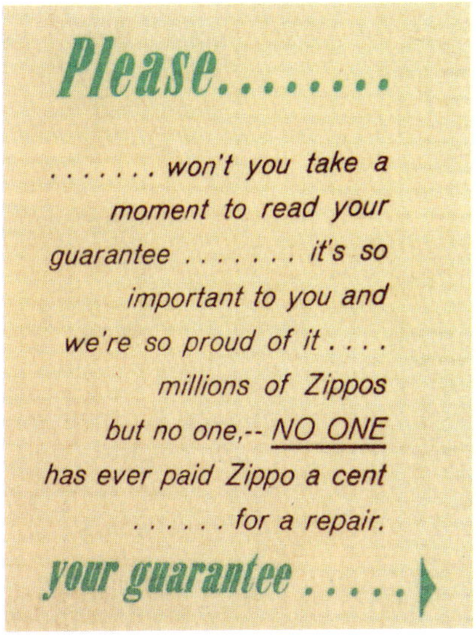

How many companies can make the same claim?

A circular sent to potential customers. Note the metalliques and the diagonal slashes.

Here is a close-up of a Gulf metallique. It is interesting that a Gulf lighter is pictured, instead of a Kendall. For this ad, a lighter was randomly pulled from the assembly line, which indicates that the Kendall lighters had already been shipped.

One of the first advertising Zippo lighters, with the Kendall logo, on display in the lobby of Zippo Manufacturing. An original, excellent condition, Kendall or Gulf lighter can fetch over $5000-6000.

From 1939. All are metalliques: the lighters are square with diagonal slashes. Also, note the Buick, Cadillac and Texaco logos.

The first full-page ad for Zippo lighters, from the December 1937 *Esquire*.

Zippo Lighter Artwork

The Advertising Beginnings

In 1935, Kendall Oil ordered 500 Zippo lighters adorned with the famous "two-thousand mile" logo. These metallique-emblemed lighters began a relationship between business and Zippo that has resulted in over 25% of today's Zippo lighter output being advertising-related. Before this order, Zippo had been focused on individual sales through stores to sportsmen and outdoorsmen.

Kendall was also located in Bradford, Pennsylvania. Bradford was, and is, a small town, and George Blaisdell made a point of knowing the other business leaders in the area. Also, because he had been in the oil business prior to the introduction of his lighter, he certainly knew the other "oil men" in the area. No one knows who first considered the advertising abilities of the "tiny tapestry" of the Zippo lighter; but, George Blaisdell immediately saw the possibility for a new and successful way to sell his lighters, and to boost the fortunes of his young company, struggling through the Depression with the rest of the United States.

The notion of a potential customer daily carrying a fashionable bit of artwork that says "buy me" was, and is, of tremendous appeal to any marketer of any product. In the market-saturated world of today, it is difficult to understand just how novel this idea was at the time. Today we buy Coke, Ford, or Chevy T-shirts, coffee mugs or pens. Baseball stadiums are named after computers or shoes, and corporate logos are everywhere we look. During the Depression, however, out-of-work men were hired to walk up and down busy city streets carrying signs that touted the virtues of this or that product.

It is no wonder then, that Zippo soon produced a pamphlet to tout the benefits of the Zippo lighter as an advertising medium. It was called "vest pocket contact" and, in addition to its historic value, it probably ranks as one of the single most accurate bits of advertising text ever written. Every word in it was and is true—even now, almost seventy years later. "Think how much it would mean if you could be the constant companion of every customer and prospect for your product. Unlike many other promotional gifts, a Zippo lighter never strays away from the man you give it to. It is his personal property, as much a part of him as his watch. (Even in 1935, the special aura of the Zippo lighter was recognized.)

The order for Kendall Oil was quickly followed by an order from Gulf. A 1935 Gulf lighter, in excellent condition, sold for $2400 in the summer of 1998 and a second, also in excellent condition, sold recently for a heart-stopping $6877. Not a bad return.

A Mack fire truck metallique.

A GMC metallique.

A superb Frigidaire metallique lighter in the Zippo Museum at the Zippo/Case Visitors Center in Bradford, Pennsylvania. Note the outside hinge.

Zippo Lighter Art Applications

The first advertising Zippo lighters used the "metallique," an extremely thin sliver of metal. A metal frame was cut to expose a silhouette of the desired lettering or artwork and attached to the case. The recesses were then color-filled. Mint condition metalliques lighters today look as if the paint is colored plastic, but it is actually an expensive lacquer. Metalliques were offered until February 1940 and are extremely valuable.

In approximately 1937, Zippo began using pantograph engraving. This process began with a pencil drawing of the proposed artwork being made on a large square of cardboard. The cardboard art was then engraved onto a brass template of about five square inches. This brass template was attached to an engraving machine, and a worker would, by hand, trace over the brass plate, thus carving the design onto as many as twelve lighters at a time. The routed out areas were then filled with paint. (The raised areas between the various colors are called "chrome-breaks.") The standard color was black. Later, other colors were available, but many of the early pantograph-engraved lighters have only black, or black and one other color—often red. As a general rule, the more colors a given bit of artwork has, the more desirable it becomes.

It was not at all uncommon for a company to reuse the same bit of artwork over several years, but change or add colors. Appropriate notations were made on the cardboards, with the changed color being noted in red pencil. This saved time and money, and one can look at a given bit of cardboard pencil art and see changes. The dates of such changes were not noted; however, it was understood that the latest variation of artwork was used on the latest batch of lighters ordered.

In the late 1940s, Zippo first offered the Town & Country series. Town & Country lighters are second in value only to the metalliques. The Town & Country process used the same method of cutting away the chrome, but without chrome breaks. Each color in the design was airbrushed into the cut out area, resulting in a one-of-a-kind painting. No two lighters were exactly alike. This type of artwork is extremely susceptible to scratches and pocket wear, and excellent condition lighters are very rare. Because there are no chrome breaks separating the colors, Town & Country lighters cannot be repainted. The last use of the T & C process was on the lighters that commemorated the 1969 moon landing. Advertising lighters using the T & C process are very rare.

ZIPPO MANUFACTURING CO.

BRADFORD, PENNSYLVANIA

New Initials!

NEW EYE APPEAL

It's happened! We have improved the personalizing of Zippo lighters by improving the initials.

Starting at once, all initials will be ENGRAVED into the lighter and INLAID with choice of red, black, blue, green or orange enamel. The former chromium letters framed with colored background are no longer available. By this improved engraving process, initials become permanently a part of the lighter.

Please note new folder attached. This is now enclosed with all Zippo lighters shipped and we feel confident you will endorse this improvement. We shall be glad to receive your comments.

Sincerely yours,

ZIPPO MANUFACTURING CO.

G. G. Blaisdell

February 1940

HCP

LDE

PCB

RNF

ZIPPO—THE WINDPROOF LIGHTER

for boating, golfing, hunting, motoring and all outdoor activities . . . or at home any place

A WEEK'S TRIAL—THEN ALL THE WHILE

A letter to the trade announcing the end of the metallique program. This letter, confirming when metallique production ended, has never before been published.

Some other, more recent, art application processes include:

Modern etch-and-Paint. This process was perfected by 1957, and allowed for more detailed designs than was possible using the pantograph. A reverse image of the artwork (like the negative of a photograph) is screened onto the case with acid-resistant paint. The lighter case is then dipped into an acid bath that etches the unprotected areas. The resulting recesses are then filled, one by one, with the correct paint.

Surface imprint. A motif is painted directly onto the surface of the lighter and then baked for durability. The case is untouched. Like T & C lighters, the artwork cannot be re-applied.

Reverse Etch. An acid application that leaves a raised logo. This is the opposite of etch & paint, with everything but the logo being acid treated. The result is unique and attractive.

Lustre Etch. An acid treatment that leaves the logo etched into the chrome. This is the same as etch & paint, but the etching is done before the case is

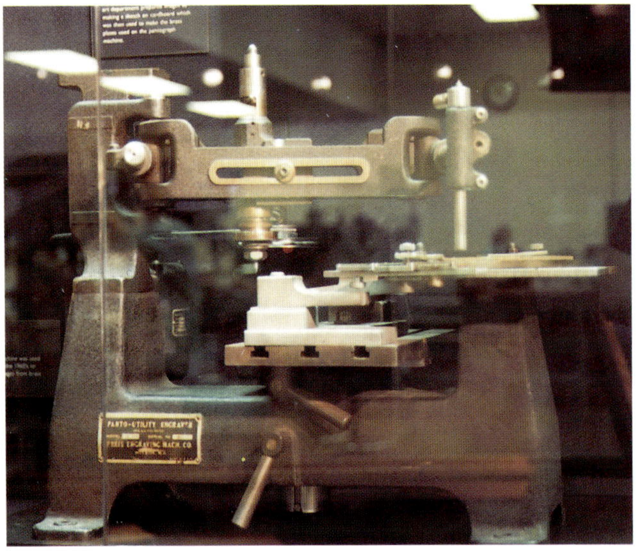

A pantograph machine, on display in the Zippo Museum.

An overhead view, showing the brass template and a lighter ready to be engraved.

A rare Town & Country Chevrolet slim lighter, from 1963. The paint has worn to the extent that only the outline of the "bowtie" logo is visible. *Courtesy Parker Collection.*

Another lighter on display in the Zippo Manufacturing lobby makes note of the etch & paint process.

plated, so the recesses are chromed and buffed to a high sheen. There is no paint applied in this process. The Mercedes series of lighters in the current Zippo lighter line are examples of the Lustre Etch process.

Etched Epoxy. The etched epoxy process combines Lustre Etch with Surface Imprint. The artwork is partially etched, the case is plated, and the balance of the artwork is screened onto the case.

Laser Engraving. This is essentially a different way of achieving the same result as Lustre Etch, but using a computer guided laser instead of an acid treatment. The result is subtle and beautiful.

Epoxy Chrome. Implemented in 1975, this involved painting the design on the brass case before chrome plating the lighter. It is no longer available.

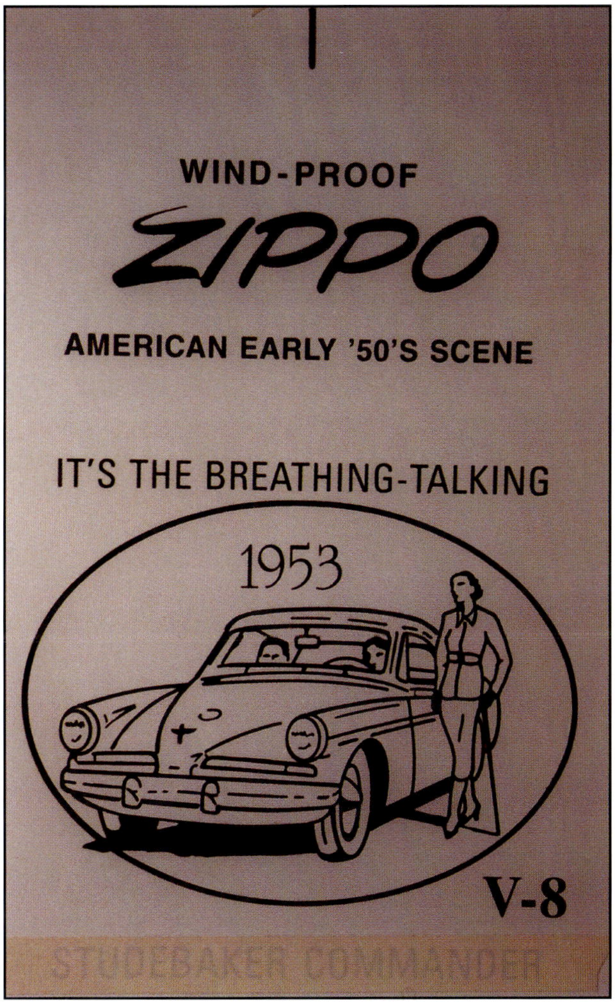

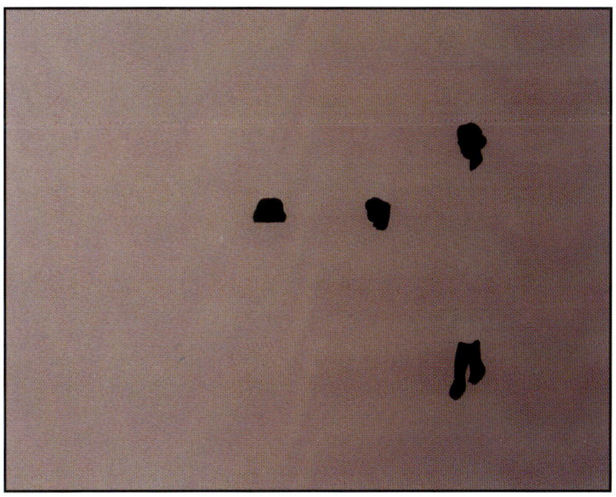

A series of photographs showing how colors are individually placed onto a lighter case. The basic design has colors added one by one, to create the final color scheme that will go onto the lighter.

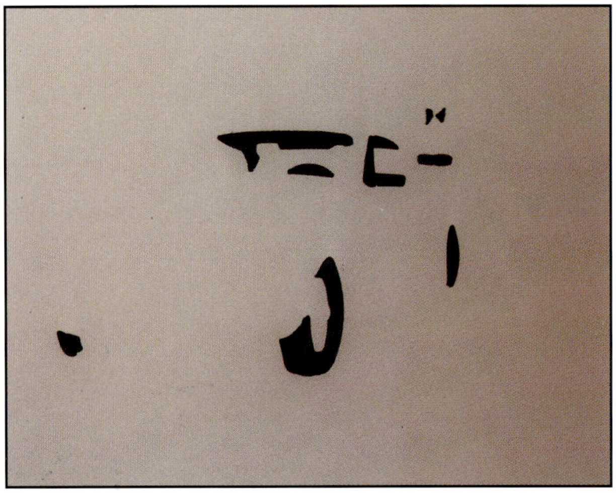

Zippo Emblems

Many companies preferred using emblems of their logos or products on Zippo lighters, instead of having them imprinted. Although the value of an emblem lighter is less than a painted counterpart, all things being equal, they are nonetheless prized.

There is a mystery to these lighters, however—one of those little sources of debate that adds spice to any collectible. Zippo did not make advertising emblems themselves. The ordering company had them made, either in-house or by a specialty company. The emblems were then sent to Zippo, where they were attached to lighters and shipped back to the company. The emblems were the responsibility of the salesman who placed the order. When the company ceased being a customer, as in the case of the independent auto makers, remaining emblems would either remain with the salesman or be discarded. The Zippo Museum has a collection of unattached emblems. Even the limited selection on display shows a vast variety of colors and logos.

Emblems can present a problem for the collector today. Fakes are not uncommon and can be difficult to detect. Almost all car companies changed their logos over the years, and knowing the correct period of a given logo can help collectors avoid being "taken." An unscrupulous person with an emblem can attach it to a lighter and then sell it as original. Recently, I found a very rare 1966 American Motors Zippo lighter for sale. The lighter was mint, the emblem, perfect. However, American Motors did not use the logo featured on that emblem until 1970, so this lighter was obviously a fake.

Another potential quandary collectors can encounter involves period-correct emblems that were attached by companies *other than* Zippo. It was not uncommon for a specialty advertising company to have emblems made and then buy a number of Zippo lighters, complete with the Zippo's deep-bottomed "emblem" box. With the Zippo lighters in hand, the emblems were then attached by that advertising company, and not by Zippo. The result is a genuine Zippo lighter, a correct company logo, and a correct box. These lighters fall into a kind of limbo, because, although genuine, they aren't fully Zippo-constructed.

Also, the emblems were not often attached effectively and they fall off easily. Because Zippo didn' t attach them in the first place, Zippo will not re-attach them. The purchaser of such a lighter is left with no recourse.

Although there is no way to guarantee that an emblem is Zippo attached, there are things to look for that can help make such a determination. Look at the lighter case around the emblem. The raised em-

A "fake" Hudson Zippo lighter. The Hudson name and logo were gone by 1963, when this lighter was made. The emblem is genuine; however, it was not put on by Zippo Manufacturing. The emblem was attached by the owner for his enjoyment. Note the difference in condition; the lighter case is pristine, though the emblem shows friction wear. *Courtesy of Ken Poynter.*

A Mack truck slim. The cutout on the chrome shows where the emblem was attached. The second picture shows the lighter after re-attachment by Zippo. $15-20

blem will protect the case finish directly around its perimeter, so a used lighter will tend to have a ring of unblemished chrome around the emblem. Next, look at the emblem itself. If it is metal, it will have a slight patina that matches the lighter itself. Look at the box, if it is present. An "emblem" Zippo lighter box will be slightly deeper than a regular box, to make room for the emblem. The emblem should also be flush against the case. Finally, make sure the logo is the one the company was using at the time the lighter was made.

Genuine emblem lighters originally had a circular cut out in the center of the chrome case, where the emblem was attached. The adhesive filled in this recess, allowing the emblem to fit flush and secure against the case. More recently made lighters do not have this cutout on the chrome. Instead, they use a very effective epoxy and super strong glue.

The epoxy is put on the center of the emblem, and glue is put on the perimeter to keep the emblem in place until the epoxy sets properly. This type of adhesive process is used on all emblem Zippo lighters today, as well as on the full-face emblems, such as the Surprise and Camel lighters. In the unlikely event that one of those emblems falls off, a look at the underside will reveal a large patch of gray, surrounded by a strip of clear. The Zippo guarantee, of course, applies to Zippo-applied emblems.

Emblems provide the Zippo collector with many potential headaches. Emblems can be delightful, however. A clean, legitimate emblem lighter should never be passed up, especially if the emblem itself has paint or is colored in some way.

This Hudson emblem lighter is obviously original. The unblemished chrome stands out clearly on the well-worn case. Even in this condition, this #203 lighter is worth $50-75.

A loose Autocar emblem on display in the Zippo Museum. This is one of the simplest types of emblems.

An extremely detailed G.M. Diesel engine emblem. Emblems representing engines or transmissions are highly detailed, but the raised areas show wear quickly, if carried regularly.

Table Lighters

The Zippo table lighter was introduced in 1938. Unlike the pocket models, the Barcroft, as it was called, had no date code and cannot be dated, though the insert can serve as a guide.

Many novice collectors are unclear as to exactly what "insert" refers to: so many, in fact, that Zippo Manufacturing actually officially changed the name of the item to "inside lighting mechanism" or "inside unit." "Insert" or "inside unit" refers to the actual "guts" of the lighter. The whole unit slides into the lighter, and is removed for refueling and for flint replacement.

The first model Barcroft was 4 1/2 inches tall, had a single step base and a special insert that had almost the same dimensions as the exterior case. The insert held an enormous amount of fuel, and was doubtless expensive to manufacture, as it was only used for these table models. The first model was discontinued because of the coming war. Another possibility for its demise, in this writer's opinion, was that it had a very high center of gravity, and, with its narrow base, wasn't very stable.

The second model Barcroft was introduced in 1947. An improvement on the first model, it was a quarter inch shorter, and had an extra step on the base. This model also used a special "full" insert, shortened to match the case. It was made until 1949.

The third model Barcoft was made available starting in 1949. The case was further shortened, to 3 1/4 inches, although it still used the expensive full insert.

The fourth, and final, Barcroft model represented a manufacturing simplification. The interior was redesigned to accept an insert from a standard pocket Zippo. The decrease in production costs made the Barcroft more profitable, though prices actually went up slightly. If the insert is original, the approximate date a Barcroft was made can be determined by looking at the insert markings.

The fourth model Barcroft was made from 1954 until 1979. It is a very heavy lighter, and its large surface was a natural for all kinds of artwork, including advertising. Barcroft table lighters with advertising are fairly common.

There were other types of Zippo table lighters made, including the Lady Bradford, the Corinthian, and the Moderne. These lighters were elegant, beautiful, delicate, and mainly intended for home use; however, some were inscribed with advertising. This group of lighters is rare and even rarer with advertising. I have never seen one with automobile advertising on it. All Zippo table lighters were discontinued by 1979.

The new generation of table lighter is called the Handilite. Introduced in the latter part of 1979, it consists of a regular pocket lighter with a heavy, stable, attached base. It is lighter than the Barcroft, easier to use, and less expensive to manufacture.

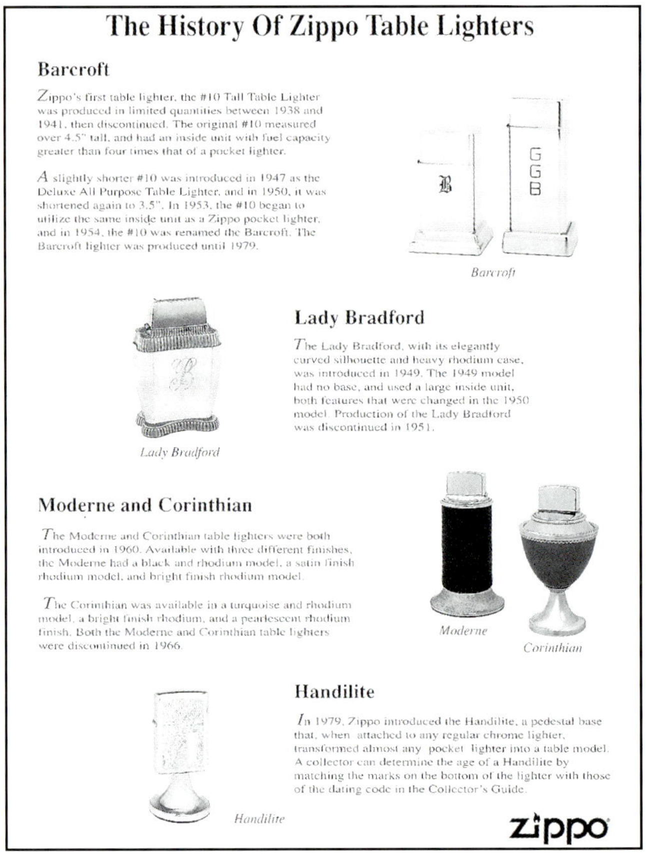

The History Of Zippo Table Lighters

Barcroft

Zippo's first table lighter, the #10 Tall Table Lighter was produced in limited quantities between 1938 and 1941, then discontinued. The original #10 measured over 4.5" tall, and had an inside unit with fuel capacity greater than four times that of a pocket lighter.

A slightly shorter #10 was introduced in 1947 as the Deluxe All Purpose Table Lighter, and in 1950, it was shortened again to 3.5". In 1953, the #10 began to utilize the same inside unit as a Zippo pocket lighter, and in 1954, the #10 was renamed the Barcroft. The Barcroft lighter was produced until 1979.

Barcroft

Lady Bradford

The Lady Bradford, with its elegantly curved silhouette and heavy rhodium case, was introduced in 1949. The 1949 model had no base, and used a large inside unit, both features that were changed in the 1950 model. Production of the Lady Bradford was discontinued in 1951.

Lady Bradford

Moderne and Corinthian

The Moderne and Corinthian table lighters were both introduced in 1960. Available with three different finishes, the Moderne had a black and rhodium model, a satin finish rhodium model, and bright finish rhodium model.

The Corinthian was available in a turquoise and rhodium model, a bright finish rhodium, and a pearlescent rhodium finish. Both the Moderne and Corinthian table lighters were discontinued in 1966.

Moderne

Corinthian

Handilite

In 1979, Zippo introduced the Handilite, a pedestal base that, when attached to any regular chrome lighter, transformed almost any pocket lighter into a table model. A collector can determine the age of a Handilite by matching the marks on the bottom of the lighter with those of the dating code in the Collector's Guide.

Handilite

Zippo

A Zippo manufacturing pamphlet about the different table lighters made through the years. The Barcroft and the Handilite are those most usually adorned with advertising. The Barcroft, with the initials G G B engraved on it, is a first model. Note the height and narrow base.

Front & back pictures of a fourth model Barcroft. This lighter has an insert from the late 1970s, so it dates from near the end of the Barcroft production. Table lighters with advertising on both sides are highly sought after. This lighter advertises a famous award from a well-known magazine. $175-200

Above: These markings inside some table lighter lids have no significance; but, note the minor carbon stains, indicating slight use.

Left: Note the unblemished chimney. All original Barcroft table lighter inserts will have an unscratched chimney, even if used. Inserts from pocket lighters will show abrasion marks over time, as the lid opens and closes.

Chrysler fourth model. *Courtesy Parker Collection.* $125-150

Chevrolet dealership fourth model Barcroft. The lines inside the logo indicate a date in the 1950s. See also the Chevrolet section. *Courtesy Parker Collection.* $200

A 1980 General Tire Handilite. Because the Handilite lighters use a standard Zippo lighter case, they are dateable. This is a very early example. $60-75

An "in-house" Buick lighter. This lighter is easier to date, because Buick went to the "tri-shield" logo in 1959. By 1964 Buick had simplified the decorations inside the individual shields. *Courtesy Parker Collection.* $125-150

A marvelous Pontiac logo, dating from before 1959. *Courtesy Parker Collection.* $125-150

The logo on this GMC lighter was used until about 1958. Therefore, this is an early fourth model Barcroft. The age and condition make this a desirable piece. $200

A dual dealership lighter with the new Pontiac logo. It was not uncommon for Cadillac dealers to also sell Pontiacs. Dealership lighters are very desirable. *Courtesy Parker Collection.* $200-250

A 1964 Ford Truck Sales lighter. *Courtesy Parker Collection.* $125-150

Polished chrome, with an older Ford logo. This is probably a very early fourth model. *Courtesy Parker Collection.* $250

An early FrigiKing fourth model. Few car buyers went to the expense of purchasing factory air-conditioning in their cars, so after-market AC systems were popular for many years. Like most "auto support" companies, this lighter is less desirable than car company examples. $100-125

Other Zippo Items

In addition to various lighters, there are other Zippo items of interest to collectors, although their values are much less than the lighters.

Zippo introduced the rule (or tape measure) in 1960. Initially, it was only an advertising item, so all of the early rules will have an advertising logo on them. This book contains the first attempt to date the Zippo Rule, a response to increasing interest in this aspect of the Zippo Phenomenon. The first rules had steel-colored tapes, with the following text printed on it:
"Zippo MADE IN U.S.A. PATENTED KEEP CLEAN LIGHTLY OILED"

The text was removed incrementally over time. By 1963, "lightly oiled" had been removed. Exactly when the rest of the text was removed is unclear, but in dating rules, the general rule-no pun intended-is, the more text on the tape, the older the rule.

By the mid-1970s, the tape itself was white, and in 1980, the bottom stamp adopted the new block letter logo with the "flame " over the "i."

The Zippo knife, available in several variations, was introduced in 1964. Here, too, is the first attempt to describe production variations of the knife. The first Zippo knife had, on the knife blade only, the following text: "Zippo BRADFORD PA USA" on three lines. The "USA" is always present, though it is sometimes obscured. The file originally had no text, but by circa 1970 it had the same text as appeared on the blade. In 1980, the blade logo adopted the "flame-over-i" logo of the rest of the Zippo line.

The Zippo magnifier, which uses the same case as the rule, was introduced in 1976.

On display in the Zippo Museum, this is a copy of the first ad for the Zippo rule. Early rules had the cursive Zippo logo on the tape itself as well as on the bottom.

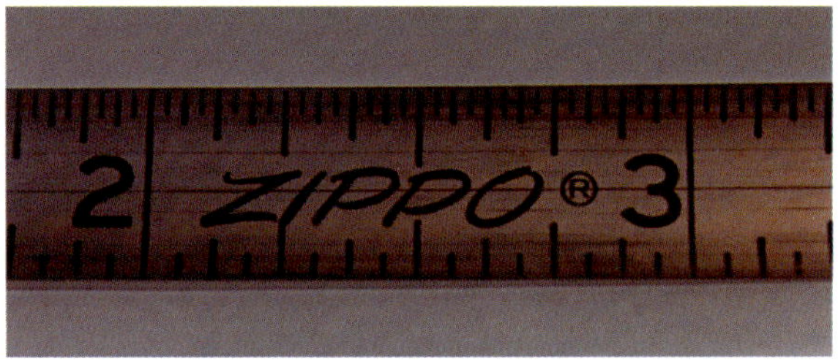

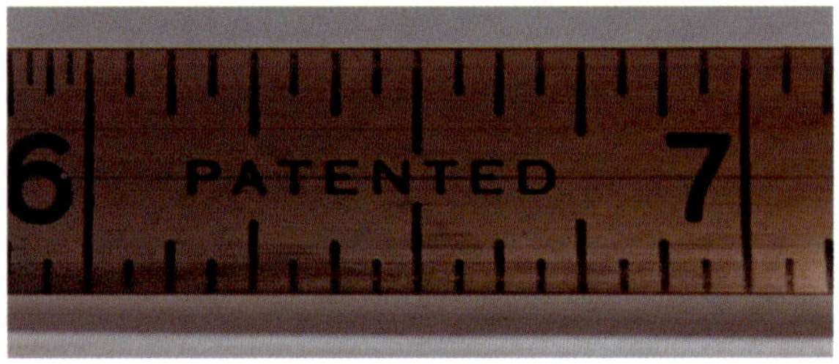

The text on the first rules. The wording was gradually removed.

Zippo also makes, or made, letter openers, pens, money clips, key chains, greenskeepers (a tool for use by golfers) and flashlights, among other things. (The Ziplight is a disposable flashlight insert that is slipped into a regular Zippo lighter case. It is also available as a complete unit, which has the Ziplight logo on it.) In 1999, Zippo began marketing watches as well.

Each of these items has its appeal, but none has the mystique of the Zippo lighter, and the value of an individual item is wholly dependent on the company advertised.

In 1980, Zippo rules adopted the "flame-over-i" logo.

This rule still has the cursive Zippo logo on the bottom; but, by this time (mid-1970s) the tape color was white and no longer had Zippo on it. $15-20 as is.

A recent rule. The bottom now has the block letter Zippo logo with the flame over the "i" and the rule comes in a plastic clamshell box. The inscription is a clever pun. $20-25

A MIB Cadillac rule from 1961. The box is stamped with the same logo as the rule itself. Cadillac items are always in demand. $85-100 with box.

Here is the other end of the scale. This rule has the same logo as the previous example, but the condition is, in a word, amazing. The Cadillac logo makes this of interest, though its value is essentially nil. *Courtesy Parker Collection.*

Here is a Ford Tractor rule. Notice the ding on the bottom right corner. *Courtesy Parker Collection.* $20-25 as is.

A lovely Rambler rule. It can be dated to circa 1963 by comparing it to 1963 Rambler lighters with the same color scheme. All Rambler items are rare. This one is mint with no box. *Courtesy Tony Zamisch.* $75-85

One of the most desirable AMC items, this mint rule dates from 1967, when AMC introduced the Javelin, for the 1968 model year. It has the same logo as a '67 lighter pictured in the AMC section. The connection to one of AMC's muscle cars makes this extremely desirable. *Courtesy Tony Zamisch.* $150

This rule has the original box, and a logo that duplicates that on a 1960 lighter pictured elsewhere in this book. The engraving was not done by Zippo Manufacturing. *Courtesy Parker Collection.* $30-35

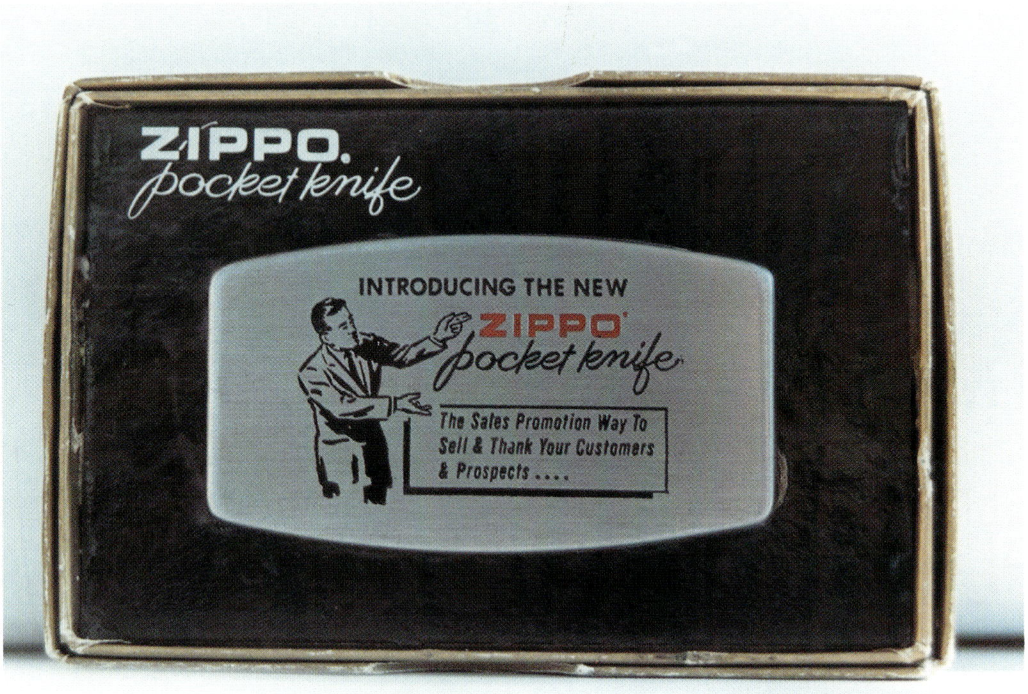

The Zippo pocket knife was new for 1964. Zippo Advertising items that advertise Zippo itself are prized, if mint in the original box. $40-50 as is without box.

This detailed artwork shows a dark green M-60 Tank with a Shillelagh missile launcher. I have the actual photo this artwork is based on and the detail is superb. Lousy weapons system, terrific knife. $40-50 with box.

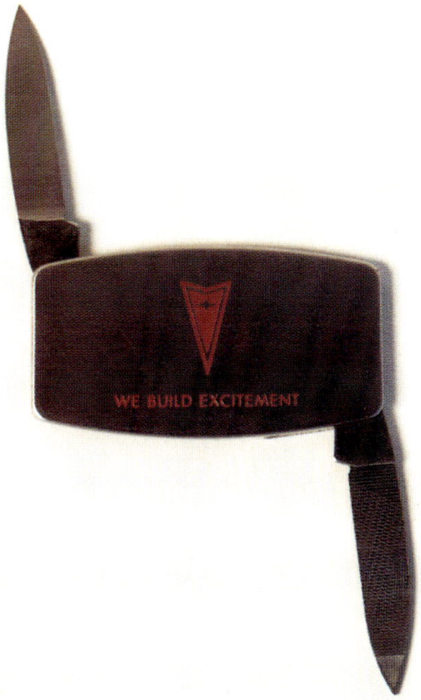

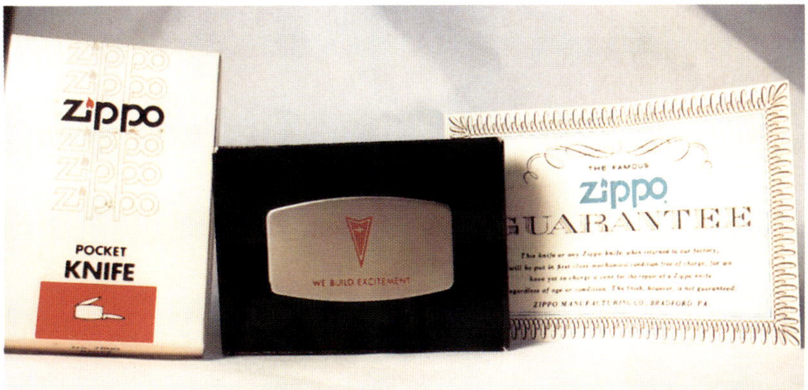

This Pontiac knife is perfect and beautiful. The ad slogan dates from the 1980s. $20-25

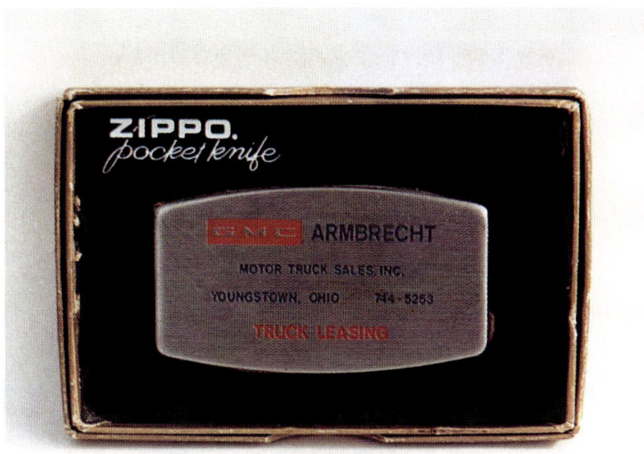

A GMC Trucks dealer. $20-25

Far left: An original Zippo Magnifier, mint in box. The magnifier used the same case as the rule. *Courtesy Parker Collection.* $15-20

Left: A Buick Magnifier showing "Happy" the hawk. *Courtesy Parker Collection.* $25-30

Dating a Zippo Lighter

The date a given Zippo lighter was made is actually less of a conundrum then many people think. From 1959 to the present, a Zippo lighter case can quickly and easily be dated to a specific year, and the insert can be dated to a specific era. The dating system used by Zippo began in mid-1955, but wasn't fully functional until 1959. The mystery lies in dating a lighter that was made before the dating system began.

George Blaisdell never intended his date code to be a service to collectors, but to customers. He wanted to increase quality control, so that if many lighters were being returned for repair, it would be possible to isolate the group within a given construction period, and more easily identify the problem.

With that in mind, it is nonetheless possible to date earlier lighters, at least within a given era. Bear in mind that silver-filled, gold-filled, 14K and 18K gold, and sterling silver lighters also were not regularly dated.

Another thing to remember about Zippo lighters is that all of them, *every single one ever made*, will have ZIPPO stamped on the bottom. Countless thousands of silver cases exist that use Zippo lighter inserts, but they are *not* Zippo lighters. Some non-Zippo lighters, notably those by Tiffany or Cartier, in sterling silver, or solid gold, are quite valuable, but they are not Zippo lighters.

The first Zippo lighters were square, with an outside hinge, and were 2 7/16 inches tall. These taller models were made only until mid-1934, when the case was shortened by 1/4 inch. So, if you find a "tall" Zippo lighter, it dates from this era, and if in mint, unrepaired condition, will probably pay for your kid's college. (I know of at least one standing offer of ten thousand dollars for a mint original "tall" Zippo lighter, and ten grand might not be enough to get it.)

Zippo made reproduction "tall" lighters, but these are easily identifiable as reproductions. They use a modern insert, and the case has filler inside to cover up the extra space.

The stamp on the bottom of Zippo lighters made until mid-1936 had PAT. PENDING stamped on them. Mid-year, the patent number 2032695 was added to the bottom, and that patent number was used until mid-1953, when a different patent number, 2517191, was put on the bottom, with "Pat. Pend." It is odd that "Pat. Pend." was also added, because patent 2517191 was issued to Zippo on August 1, 1950.

There is considerable debate as to exactly when the following changes occurred, but there is no disagreement that each change is mentioned in sequential order. Dated cardboards will eliminate most, if not all, the questions about when a specific bottom stamp was used.

In mid-1955, the famous "dots" were added. This year marks the beginning of the date code. The logic was to have a series of eight symbols on the lighter, and each year remove one symbol. When the last symbol was removed, the next year would see another "era" with a different set of symbols. This is quite simple and effective, but there were some alterations to the bottom that make the date code confusing.

The first "dot" code was eight symbols, and the bottom of the lighter also had, on the left, 2517191, and on the right, "PAT. PEND." A lighter with these markings dates from the second half of 1955.

In 1956, one dot was removed from the left, and all else remained the same. Because the patent had already been issued to Zippo, "PAT. PEND" was superfluous and, in 1957, the "PAT. PEND." was removed. The patent number remained on the left side of the case, however. The dot that had been removed in 1956 *returned*, so a lighter with eight dots and a left-side "Pat. 2517191" is a 1957 lighter.

Confused? It gets better, and that can be taken two ways.

In 1958, "PAT. 2517191" was centered, and there were *still* eight dots. *Then*, by 1959, the far left dot was again removed, and the date code was fully in effect, with a single dot removed for each year.

In 1966, a new series of markings began, consisting of eight vertical lines. Each year a line was removed, so that a 1973 Zippo lighter will have only one "line."

The next symbol used, from 1974-1981, was the "forward slash." Again, eight slashes were used to start, with one symbol being removed for each year.

Then came the "backward slashes." This dating symbol began in 1982, but only continued until mid-1986, when the current date code began. The new code was designed so that the month of manufacture, as well as the year, could be identified. It consists of a letter (A-L) on the left side of the bottom of the lighter, which designates the month from January-December, and a Roman numeral on the right bottom, designating the year. For reasons known only to Zippo (and perhaps not even to them), the Roman numeral code began with II. I have seen at least one Zippo lighter dated F II, or June 1986, so presumably, the Roman system was in effect by May 1986, which makes 1986 lighters dated \\ZIPPO\\ uncommon.

So, when looking at the bottom of a Zippo case, look first for the patent number. If it has *only* "PAT. PENDING", in addition to the Zippo name, it was made from 1933 until mid-1936, when the "PAT. PENDING" was changed to "PAT. 2032695."

If the lighter has 2032695 on the bottom, it dates from 1936 to mid-1953.

If the lighter has 2517191 on the bottom, it dates from mid-1953 to 1967, when "PAT. 2517191" was removed. Issued August 1, 1950, patent 2517191 expired in August 1967. Lighters dating from 1953 can be found with both patent numbers (2032695 and 2517191). Buick and Ford each celebrated fifty-year anniversaries in 1953, and each company plastered just about every 1953 product they offered to the public with anniversary logos. Because the new car model year began in October, ad campaigns were usually planned in the spring. Therefore, orders for Zippo advertising lighters would have been placed as early as the previous June. A lighter with a 1953 Anniversary marking or emblem, then, would actually have been produced between circa June 1952

Zippo LIGHTER IDENTIFICATION CODES

YEAR	REGULAR		SLIM	
	LEFT	RIGHT	LEFT	RIGHT
1933	Patent Pending			
1937	Patent 2032695			
1942-1946	Black Crackle, Patent 203695 (This number was stamped in error, it should have been Patent 2032695)			
c.1949-c.1957	Patent 2517191 with patent pending			

Zippo records indicate an overlap of bottom stamp configurations from 1949-1957. Also, some lighters produced between 1955-57 were date coded, however, specifics remain unclear. The date coding was fully in effect by 1959.

YEAR	REGULAR LEFT	REGULAR RIGHT	SLIM LEFT	SLIM RIGHT
c.1951-c.1957	Patent 2517191			
1957			....	....
1958	Patent 2517191		....	....
	....	....	....	...
1959	....	...	...	...
1960	...	...	...	..
1961	...	..	..	..
1962	..	..	..	.
1963	..	.	.	.
1964	.	.	.	
1965	.			
1966	IIII	IIII	IIII	IIII
1967	IIII	III	IIII	III
1968	III	III	III	III
1969	III	II	III	II
1970	II	II	II	II
1971	II	I	II	I
1972	I	I	I	I
1973	I		I	
1974	////	////	////	////

YEAR	REGULAR		SLIM	
	LEFT	RIGHT	LEFT	RIGHT
1975	////	///	////	///
1976	///	///	///	///
1977	///	//	///	//
1978	//	//	//	//
1979	/	//	//	/
1980	/	/	/	/
1981	/		/	
1982	\\\\	\\\\	\\\\	\\\\
1983	\\\\	\\\	\\\\	\\\
1984	\\\	\\\	\\\	\\\
1985	\\\	\\	\\\	\\
1986	\\	\\	\\	\\

Effective 7-1-86 the above system was replaced by year lot code. Year is noted with roman numeral letter designates lot month (A=Jan., B=Feb., etc.)

	REGULAR & SLIM	
1986	G to L	II
1987	A to L	III
1988	A to L	IV
1989	A to L	V
1990	A to L	VI
1991	A to L	VII
1992	A to L	VIII
1993	A to L	IX
1994	A to L	X
1995	A to L	XI
1996	A to L	XII
1997	A to L	XIII
1998	A to L	XIV
1999	A to L	XV
2000	A to L	XVI

Visit zippo.com to see the date codes for the 21st century, starting with the year 2001.

The free dating guide provided by Zippo Mfg. Note the vague information about lighters made before 1959.

and June 1953. Basically, this means that just because lighter artwork refers to a specific year does not mean it was made *in* that year.

Another feature of a Zippo lighter case that can help narrow the year of manufacture is the hinge. Early Zippo lighter cases had an outside three-barrel hinge. Both the hinge and the hinge plates attaching the hinge to the case were mounted on the outside of the case. This three-barrel hinge was used until mid-1936, when a fourth barrel was added to the external hinge.

From 1937-1942, a four-barrel hinge was used, but the hinge plates were moved to the inside of the lighter. Only the hinge itself remained visible from the outside.

In 1943, Zippo returned to the three-barrel hinge (with internal hinge plates), using this hinge until early 1950. Then a thick five-barrel hinge was adopted and used until mid-1956, when a thin five-barrel hinge was adopted. The thin five-barrel hinge has been used ever since.

Therefore, if a lighter has a three-barrel outside attached hinge, it was made from 1933 until sometime in 1936.

There are reproduction "outside hinge" lighters; however, these actually have five-barrel inside hinges, with fake side plates on the outside. A look inside the case will easily identify a reproduction.

If a lighter has a four-barrel outside attached hinge, it was made briefly in 1936. If a lighter has an inside four-barrel hinge, it was made from 1937 to 1942. If a lighter had an inside three-barrel hinge, it was made from 1943 to about 1950.

The case itself changed shape over the years. Early cases, from 1933 until 1936, were square-cornered. Rounded cases were introduced in 1937. So, if you have an original square-cornered lighter (again, there are reproduction square-cornered lighters), it was made from 1933-1936. The bottom of the round-cornered lighters is slightly pushed out.

Therefore, if you have a lighter without the date codes on the bottom, it is fairly easy to narrow down its era by observing the features listed above. The hinge, patent number, and case, taken in their various combinations, will allow for a fairly precise dating of the era of manufacture.

Zippo Canada was opened in 1949 in an effort to avoid paying Canadian import duties. Canadian-made Zippo lighters have no date code at all. The case and insert were—and are—made in Bradford, then trucked to Canada and stamped with Canadian markings. The Canadian branch of Zippo employs only twenty-eight people, and Canadian Zippo lighters are rare.

The bottom of an early Canadian Zippo lighter case has the following stamp:

ZIPPO MFG. CO. CANADA, LTD.
PATENTED ZIPPO 1950
(The word "ZIPPO" was slightly larger
than the rest of the text)
NIAGARA FALLS, ONTARIO

By 1963, Canadian bottom stamps had removed the year "1950," though exactly when is unclear. Because the slim lighter bottom is so much smaller than the full-size lighters, Canadian slim cases have no special marking.

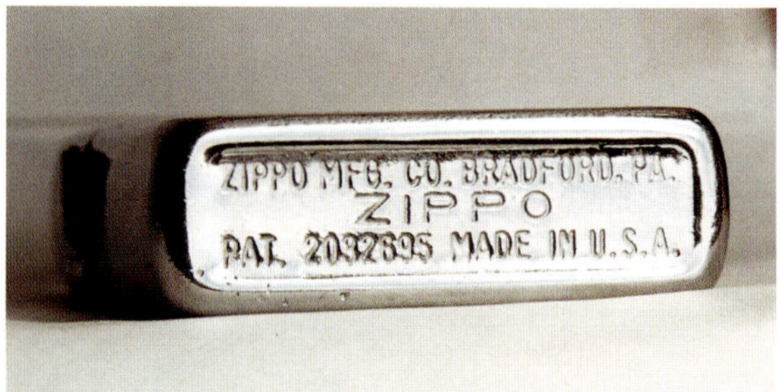

Note the #203 stamp, but a five-barrel hinge. This lighter is mint. *All lighters pictured in this section are courtesy Parker Collection.* $150-175

Sterling silver or gold cases were not usually dated.

A mint 1951 Suggestion Winner.

The logo has changed very slightly. Also, the bottom stamp is not as deeply struck. This lighter was made before mid-1953.

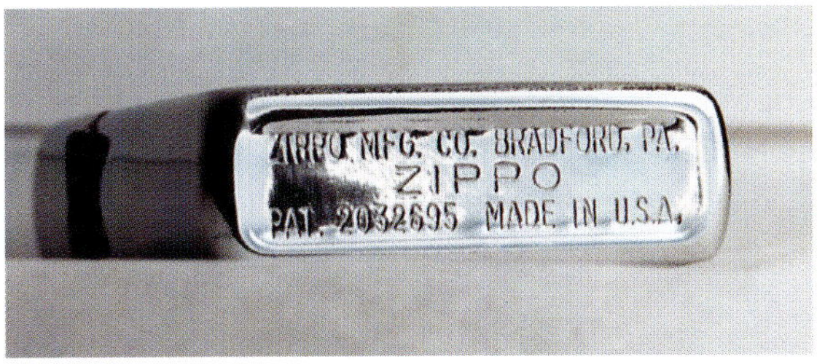

A very early 2517191 stamp. The lighters were ordered about 6 weeks prior to the date stamped on the lighter, which is an indication of when the change in bottom stamps occurred.

The full 2517191 stamp.

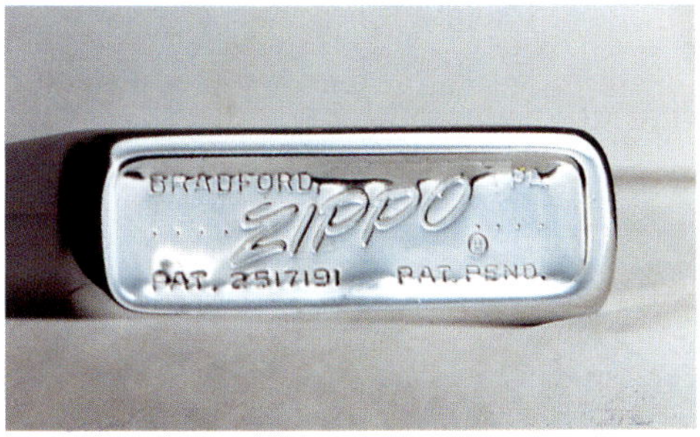

The thicker text underneath the logo is the only difference between this lighter and the 1954 example. This is the first of the "dot" stamps, with both PAT. 2517191 and Pat Pend.

Notice one dot missing from the left, with all else the same.

These 1956 lighters both have the same bottom stamp, but one has the modern "thin five-barrel" hinge.

The dot has returned, and PAT PEND has been removed. Car model years started in the fall, so orders for advertising items would be placed and filled as early as the July before the new model year.

This is a 1958 lighter. During this period, stamps were changed mid-year, and orders for car lighters were made way in advance. As a result, there are two different stamps for each year from 1953-1959.

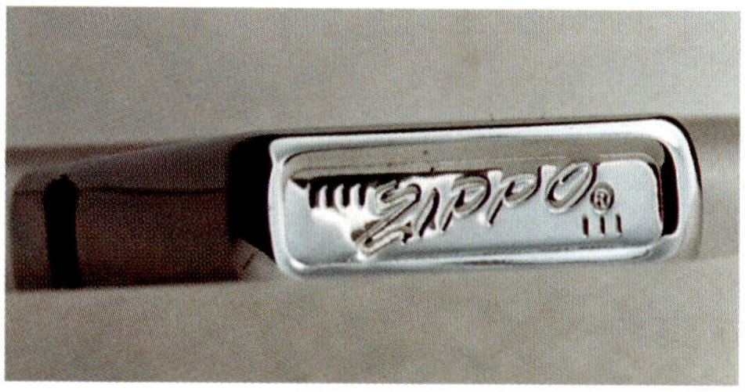

This lighter shows how advance orders for the approaching model year can result in discrepancies between the year of the lighter and the year stated on the case. This is a 1968 Suggestion Winner lighter, yet the date stamped on the case is 1967.

This lighter has the "correct" date of 1966 on the case.

Inserts

Inserts can also be dated, and a mint Zippo lighter should always have its correct insert. The 1933 inserts were 1 5/8 inches and had no markings on them. When the case was shortened a quarter inch, the inserts were as well.

When Zippo moved the hinge plates to the inside of the case in 1936, the insert was fractionally narrowed to make room for the hinge. The cam (the pivoting arm that holds a lighter closed) used a coiled spring to maintain tension, and this spring weakened very quickly; so, in 1937 a flat spring replaced the coiled one. Most coil spring inserts were repaired or replaced, and units in original condition are extremely rare.

The Chimney and flint wheel are also dating aids. The first inserts had sixteen holes in the chimney. Circa 1936, that number was reduced to fourteen, when the bottom left hole was removed on each side. In circa 1947, Zippo once more began making inserts with sixteen hole-chimneys, and still does today. So, if you have a fourteen-hole chimney, the insert was made between circa 1936-circa 1947. (Because such alterations were made as running changes, "circa" is a commonly used word in discussions about Zippo lighters.)

The flint wheel itself underwent a major change as well. The flint wheel teeth were originally horizontal. In about 1946, angled teeth were adopted, and the material used to make the flint wheel was changed.

Inserts from "2032695" lighters have the patent number stamped horizontally across the bottom, in addition to "ZIPPO MFG. CO. BRADFORD, PA." and "MADE IN ZIPPO USA." Early "2517191" inserts are stamped horizontally across the bottom, but they also have "PAT. PEND." stamped on them. "PAT. PEND." was removed in 1957, although the stamping still ran horizontally across the bottom of the insert. In 1958, the patent number was moved from the left of the insert to the center, as on the case.

In late 1958, "FOR BEST RESULTS USE ZIPPO FLINTS AND FLUID" was added above the patent number. This insert was produced for less then a year. In late 1959, the wording was relocated to run vertically up the side of the lighter, so that when the insert was removed for re-fueling, the user would see a reminder to "use Zippo flints and fluid."

A typical full-stamp #251 insert, including the PAT.PEND. This insert dates from circa 1956.

The PAT. PEND has been removed, though the patent number is still on the left.

This post-1967 insert lacks the patent number, but has the "for best results.." text added late in 1958. The text runs across the side on this example, as it has since 1959.

These inserts are typical Canadian examples. They are both earlier than about 1963, by which time the "1950" had been removed.

This insert was used until August 1967, when the patent number was removed. From 1968-1975, the only wording on the insert was:

"FOR BEST RESULTS USE ZIPPO FLINTS
AND FLUID,"<br>"ZIPPO MFG CO. BRADFORD, PA."
"MADE IN ZIPPO USA"

In 1976, the "warning label" inserts appeared, with the following warnings on the reverse:

"LIGHTER DOES NOT
SELF-EXTINGUISH"
"CLOSE LID TO PUT IT OUT"
"KEEP AWAY FROM CHILDREN
"AFTER FILLING WIPE LIGHTER
& HANDS BEFORE LIGHTING"

In 1982, Zippo began dating inserts with the same date code as on their cases. When the Roman numeral code began, the inserts were also dated with the month, as well as the year. It is actually uncommon to find a Zippo lighter with an insert from the same month. Almost all "Roman" system Zippo lighters I have seen have an insert that dates from two to three months before or after the month on the case. The slim inserts follow the same pattern as the full size lighters, although 1956 inserts have an odd shield in front of the flint wheel. The purpose of the "wheel guard," as it was called, was to keep the flint wheel from becoming too hot. It was useless, and not very many made it to consumers. In 1957, "wheel guard" inserts had the guards removed and future inserts lacked them. "Wheel guard" slim Zippo lighters are uncommon.

The Canadian insert had the exact same text running horizontally across the bottom of the insert. Later inserts adopted the same markings as the American ones.

Restoration

In broad terms, people who own Zippo cigarette lighters can be separated into two groups: users and collectors. Each group values Zippo lighters for the same reasons, but the collector group is an extension of the user group. Collectors are people who began collecting Zippo lighters because of their indescribable appeal.

The collector is interested in Zippo lighters that are original in all their components: insert, hinge, paint, condition, paperwork, labels and package. The user is interested in having a lighter that is as attractive and efficient as possible. The terms "user" and "collector" could also be applied to lighters themselves: lighters used daily, and lighters that will not even be handled. With this thought in mind, how much restoration is acceptable, and how much is going "too far" in terms of maintaining value?

The finish is neither guaranteed nor replaceable by Zippo Manufacturing. A "brassed" lighter—one with the chrome plating partially worn off—cannot be re-plated. There are, however, many things that can be done at the owner's discretion.

When a lighter is sent back to Zippo for repair, the following things are done to it, unless the sender makes specific requests. The lighter is re-hinged. (The old, wobbly hinge is removed and a new one is attached.) The inside lighting mechanism is replaced with a new one (although the old one is returned unaltered, even if it is crushed or corroded into uselessness.) If included with the lighter, emblems are re-attached if they have fallen off. *Zippo does not have replacement emblems in stock; the original must be returned with the lighter.* For a small charge, the color artwork will be re-painted, if desired and if possible, depending on the type of color application process originally used.

A Zippo lighter can be returned to an almost new condition, with new hinge, inside lighting mechanism, and paint. Only the finish cannot be altered. But should it be done? Unlike car collectors, for whom a correct and well-done restoration helps rather than harms a vehicle's value, most lighter collectors cringe at the thought of *any* change from the original. Some restorations are not possible anyway.

The various hinges used from 1943-present. All Zippo lighters have used the "thin" five-barrel hinge since mid-1956.

Note the difference in wicks. The longer wick is the older type. The other wick is the later style, with extremely fine wire visible in the weave.

For instance, a Zippo lighter with a three, four, or thick five-barrel hinge returned to Zippo will be fitted with a modern thin five-barrel hinge. Not too much of a concern for a user, perhaps, but the kiss of death for most collectors. A rare and valuable old Zippo that has a wobbly hinge should be retired to display duty unchanged. Restoring it will almost ensure that collectors will pass it by unless it fills a gap in a collection, and then the value will be only a fraction of what it would have been if left unmodified.

Some users replace the hinge pin itself. Knocking out the worn-out hinge pin and replacing it with a section of a paper clip tightens the hinge very nicely, although it usually looks awful, and again, will dissuade most collectors.

A better alternative, when possible, is to send the lighter to Zippo, with written instructions to replace the hinge pin only. This can be done unless one or more of the barrels of the hinge is broken. This repair can only be made, however, on lighters with a thin five-barrel hinge.

I have had some old lighters re-painted, purely for my own enjoyment, but I have done so with the knowledge that the value of these lighters is damaged, and that many collectors are not interested in trading for or buying them. However, I plan to keep them, and the loss of value is less important to me personally than the increased beauty, which, after all, is in the eye of the beholder.

I have several other Zippo lighters, however, which will not be repainted. They will remain as they are for one of several reasons, either because of their rarity or value as they are, or because the case is worn enough that repainting would look silly and out of place. Also, the type of paint used over the years has changed. A lighter that was originally Yale blue, for instance, would still be painted Yale blue, were it sent back for a repaint, but the color would be a slightly different shade than the original.

Comparing a mint original to a repainted duplicate, it is usually possible to see the difference between the various paints. Most experts can tell, without comparing, whether a lighter has been repainted. If you are considering buying a high-dollar lighter, and you are not sure if the paint is original, try to find another lighter to compare with your potential purchase. Most dealers will say that a lighter has been repainted, but buyers should nonetheless use caution before plunking down a pile of dough for a lighter. The general rule of thumb is: don't alter a lighter unless you are going to keep it. If it's a keeper, well, then, have fun. But if you ever plan to sell or trade it, don't change a thing.

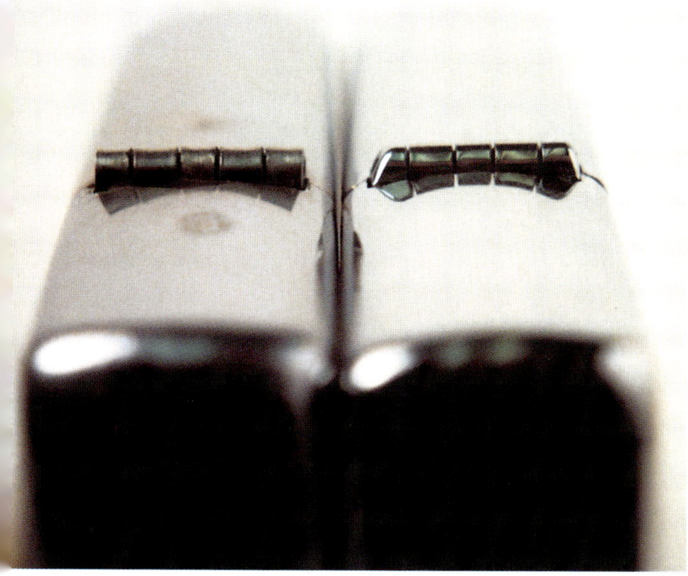

An original hinge is beveled and chromed: a replacement hinge is neither.

This Nash lighter has been re-hinged at least once. The thin hinge leaves open space where the original thicker hinge had been, and the shiny new hinge sticks out badly. It looks unpleasant, to say the least. Note the upper weld point. $50-60 as is.

This 1956 "Wisconsin Air-Cooled Engines" lighter was sent to Zippo with a crushed lid and insert. Fitted with a replacement lid and insert, it now works perfectly. Such a restoration returns value to a cherished item, and because the logo was neither damaged, nor re-done, it may still have collector value. This logo has also been found on early Barcroft table lighters. $20-25 as is.

The blemish caused by failure to remove the flint before storage. This flint was removed before totally cementing to the flint wheel, and this corrosion can be carefully cleaned off. Marred flint wheels are common and reduce value up to 30%.

This flint has completely frozen to the wheel, and must be very carefully drilled out. Because lighters were usually stored with the flint in the flint tube, frozen flint wheels are very common, as is "insert-switching." Many collectors buy mint plain lighters just to get an insert with an unfrozen wheel.

The full-size FrigiKing lighter is mint original, whereas the slim has been re-painted. The difference is easily seen. Slim: $20-30; full-size: $100-125.

Re-painting has vastly improved the appearance of this 1963 "Phillips 66" lighter, though its value is reduced. A close look will reveal a thinning of the chrome on the lower left front of the case. $15-20 as is.

The left lighter has been re-painted, whereas the right one is mint. Notice the difference in the brightness and evenness of the red. Left: $30-40; right: $60-75

Values

This book is dealing with a subset of a specific type of Zippo lighters (ie. Zippo lighters, advertising, automotive). The prices listed here only apply to that subset of Zippo lighters.

There are four things to consider when gauging the value of a Zippo lighter: age, condition, company, and type of artwork. The collectible value of a Zippo lighter decreases drastically with youth. A rule of thumb is that old Zippo lighters are more valuable as Zippo lighters and newer ones are more desirable as symbols of a given company, up to the "Roman" era (when the date code began using Roman numerals instead of symbols), when values flatten out into the "retail" category. There are spikes of value, however, where a specific piece has value beyond the norm. Examples would include gold or sterling silver cases (extremely rare, given that these are essentially give-away items), Tucker and Edsel lighters, or final year examples.

Some car companies have two final years; 1958 was the last year Packard cars were made, for example, but 1956 saw the last true Packards. The artwork is last for a simple reason: when given more detail then simple black line art, well, beauty *is* in the eye of the beholder. Some collectors dislike emblems, some covet Town & Country lighters, others love complex art, and some like as many colors as possible. Most Zippo ad lighters have from one to three colors, with black, red, and blue dominating. Professionally done engraving has a negligible effect, if any, on values. Hand-carved serial numbers or names, however, can easily throw an otherwise fine lighter into the category of "filler." *If present, however, these home-made marks should not be removed*. I have seen some otherwise fine Zippo lighters hopelessly marred by an attempt to remove an unwanted marking.

Looking through this book will give the reader an idea of just how rare lighters are that advertise the independents. Chevrolet lighters illustrated here, for instance, outnumber all the independent examples put together. Unless its condition borders on horrible, a Hudson, Nash or Packard lighter will always be more desirable then a Chevrolet lighter.

Prices fluctuate. There are fads, price explosions and burnouts. I like Hudson, Nash, and so on, so I would happily pay, or trade, a lot more for one of these than for, say, a perfect #251 Cadillac (such a lighter would date from mid-1953-1957). Many people nowadays think of Hudson as a bay, Packard as a computer, and Nash as a misspelling of what you do with your teeth when you're frustrated. They care less about such lighters, though they might be eager for a nice #203 Chevrolet. Most collectors would rather trade than buy or sell anyway, as the "trading game" is part of the pleasure of the hobby. Therefore, this is a guide only.

This guide is broken up into eras named after the *dominant identifier* of that era. It omits prices for the earliest Zippo lighters, which are outside the scope of this book. Because the metallique ended in 1940, it is convenient to speak of the first "era" as being the metallique era, 1935-1940. The "four-barrel" era includes the rounded lighters made from 1937-1942, so a round lighter has its own value, even if it might be older then a metallique. A four-barrel metallique is still included in the "metallique era" because it is the metallique that is the *dominant identifier*. The #203 "era" lighters are those from 1943-1953. Even though lighters were stamped with #203 starting in 1936, the number of barrels gives those earlier lighters their name. A collector would say, "I have a four-barrel outside hinge" or " I have a four-barrel inside hinge." That same collector would also say, "I have a #203 three-barrel" if he is referring to a lighter made between 1943-50. There is no distinction between a #203 three-barrel and a #203 five barrel, so I have placed them in the same era.

The #251 era refers to those lighters made from mid-1953-1957, even though "dots" showed up in 1955. The "dot" era is from 1958-1965 when the date code was fully in effect, and so on. I have made one chart for all American car makes. *All prices shown in the table are for full-size mint examples*, except for the metalliques and four-barrel eras. The values mentioned in the captions reflect the approximate value of a lighter in "as pictured" condition. Thus, the collector will have a guide to mint and used lighters. Note that all the metalliques have the same value. Those are old enough, and rare enough, that condition is a minor factor. Deductions for condition, added engraving, etc., are up to the buyer, although I have included a visual guide to colors, emblems, and brassing. Note that modern era values tend to flatten out at around $40. A new, decorated Zippo lighter costs from $25-35, so I am factoring in slightly more for the company logo.

A word about terms; there are really only three terms that have concrete definitions in the Zippo lighter collecting field:

Mint In Box, or MIB, means exactly that: perfect. No blemishes, a correct insert, complete paperwork, an unblocked flint tube, and an unfrozen flint wheel. There is no such thing as "mint except for..." MIB lighters are very rare as most were stored with flints, which cemented to the wheel and flint tube over time.

Mint, no box. This means a lighter is exactly as above, but without a box or paperwork. These lighters are even more rare, because the box protects the finish and removing a mint lighter from the box makes it vulnerable to scratching, even if stored carefully.

Unused. This term means the lighter has not been used, though it has blemishes. Not enough to hurt the beauty, but *not* mint. Many lighters called "mint" are actually "unused." (If an insert switch is suspected, look inside the lid for carbon accumulation. An unused lighter lid will be shiny inside, regardless of age.) As I wrote this book, it was annoying to have to downgrade many of the lighters in my own collection; but, mint is mint, and there's no getting around it.

The overwhelming majority of used lighters can be graded using a percentage system, based on how much paint is left in the artwork. Generally, the overall condition will be reflected in the condition of the logo.

This chart refers only to full-size Zippo lighters.

Fourth model Barcrofts have a base value of $125-150. Add an additional $50 for each previous model, to the rare first model Barcroft, which is worth up to $1000.

Advertising Handlite lighters are $75-100.

Slim lighters are valued between $30-40. Company and condition are much more important with slims.

Multiple colors and complex art add value, as does verifiable Canadian origin.

Emblems, re-hinging, incorrect inserts, and single-color text-only ads subtract value. An incorrect insert or one with a frozen flint wheel or blocked flint tube subtracts as much as 30%. Missing paperwork does not seem to affect values, although an absent box does, slightly. Non-lighter Zippo items are worth much less and are covered in their section.

Zippo Manufacturing does not *determine the collector value of* any *product it makes.*

Caring For Your Zippo Lighter

Whether a Zippo is purchased for use, or for display as a bit of Americana, it should be cared for in approximately the same way.

Name	1935-1940 Metallique	1936-1942 Four-barrel	1943-1953 #203	1953-1957 #251
AMC/Rambler	N.A.	N.A.	N.A.	N.A.
Bricklin	N.A.	N.A.	N.A.	N.A.
Hudson	Unknown. If found, $1000-1200	Unknown. If found, $400+	$300-350	$250-350 Last true Hudson December 29, 1954
International Harvester	unknown	unknown	$125-150	$125-150
Jeep	N.A.	N.A.	Unknown	Unknown
Kaiser-Frazer	N.A.	N.A.	$200-300	$200-250
Nash	Unknown. If found, $1000-1200+	Unknown. If found, $400+	$250-350	$150-175 Merge with Hudson May 1, 1954
Mack	$1000-1200	$400-600	$200-300	$150-175
Packard	Unknown. If found, Ask the man who owns one.	Unknown. See previous	$250-350	$200-300 Merged with Studebaker, June 22, 1954
Studebaker	$1000-1200+	$400+	$200-300	$200-300
Tucker	N.A.	N.A.	$1000-1200	N.A.
White	$1000-1200	$400+	$200-300	$150-175
Reo	$1000-1200	$400+	$200-300	$100-125
Diamond T	$1000-1200	$400+	$200-300	$100-125
Chevrolet	$1000-1200	$400+	$200-300	$150-175
Pontiac	$1000-1200	$400+	$200-300	$150-175
Buick	$1000-1200	$400+	$200-300	$150-175
Oldsmobile	$1000-1200	$400+	$200-300	$150-175
Cadillac	$1000-1200	$400+	$200-300	$150-175
GMC	$1000-1200	$400+	$200-300	$150-175
Ford	$1000-1200	$400+	$200-300	$150-175 Edsel $400-450
Lincoln	$1000-1200	$400+	$200-300	$150-175
Mercury	$1000-1200	$400+	$200-300	$150-175
Zephyr	$1200-1500	$400+ Zephyr discontinued 1941	N.A.	N.A.
Chrysler	$1000-1200	$400+	$200-300	$150-175
Plymouth	$1000-1200	$400+	$200-300	$150-175
Dodge	$1000-1200	$400+	$200-300	$150-175
DeSoto	$1000-1200	$400+	$200-300	$150-175

All labels should be removed, carefully. There are some collectors who prefer to leave labels in place. However, the longer a label is left on a lighter, the more likely it is that the adhesive will discolor the chrome, so that when the label *is* removed, there will be a spot where it had been. Use a hairdryer set on warm to loosen the adhesive, and gently peel off the label, but do *not* discard it. The label is part of the packaging, and it should be kept with the lighter. The best thing to do with a removed label is to just stick it on the inside of the box. That way it won't be lost, and it can always be replaced, if desired.

Flints should always be removed from a lighter that is not going to see use. The flint oxidizes over time, and will solidify within the flint tube. It is not uncommon to find "frozen" flint wheels and blocked flint tubes. In such cases, the flint must be carefully drilled out, and there will remain a residue that mars the appearance of an otherwise pristine lighter.

Brass lighters should be cleaned with Brasso or a non-abrasive polish, although some collectors simply use lighter fluid itself, very gently polishing the case with fluid and a cloth. Do *not* use any paper products to polish a lighter. Paper is made of wood, and the microscopic wood fibers in paper, even tissue paper, will scratch the case, especially if it is polished chrome. Synthetic fabric, especially polyester, is also to be avoided.

If a lighter is purchased with the original box and paperwork, but it will be displayed, the box and paperwork should be safely stored, because the box is part of the total package. If the box is damaged or lost, it affects the value of the lighter. When I separate a box from the attendant lighter, I write on a scrap piece of paper what lighter goes with that box, and store that little note inside the box. Doing that allows me to keep box and lighter together, without making any markings on the box itself.

If lighters are carried on a daily basis, try to get in the habit of keeping a lighter in a pocket by itself, and put the debris of daily life in the other pocket. The little coin pocket on the right side of a pair of jeans is a perfect place to carry a Zippo lighter.

1958-1965 "dots"	**1966-1973 "lines"**	**1974-1981 "forward-slash"**	**1982-1986 "backward-slash"**	**June 1986-Present "Roman"**
$150-175	$100-125	$150-175 A Javelin/AMX lighter would far exceed this.	$75-100	$50-75 Last American independent car, made December 14, 1987.
N.A.	N.A.	$100-150 Slim $75-100	N.A.	N.A.
$200-300 Hudson name discontinued after '57 model year	N.A.	N.A.	N.A.	N.A.
$75-100	$40-60	$40-60	$40-60	$30-40
Unknown	$50-75 AMC purchased Jeep February 1970	$50-75	$50-75	$150-175 if AMC/ Jeep. If Chrysler, $30-40
N.A.	N.A.	N.A.	N.A.	N.A.
200-300 Nash name discontinued after '57 model year	N.A.	N.A.	N.A.	N.A.
$50-75	$30-40	$30-40 Common	$30-40 Common	$30-40 Common
$200-300 Last true Packard made August 15, 1956 Packard name discontinued 1958	N.A.	N.A.	N.A.	N.A.
$100-125	$200-300 Studebaker dies, 1966	N.A.	N.A.	N.A.
N.A.	N.A.	N.A.	N.A.	N.A.
$100-125				N.A.
$100-125	N.A.	N.A.	N.A.	N.A.
$100-125	$50-75	N.A.	N.A.	N.A.
$100-125	$50-75	$40-50	$30-40 Common	$30-40 Common
$100-125	$50-75	$40-50	$40-50	$40-50
$100-125	$50-75	$40-50	$40-50	$40-50
$100-125	$50-75	$40-50	$40-50	$40-50
$100-125	$50-75	$40-50	$40-50	$40-50
$100-125	$50-75	$40-50	$40-50	$40-50
$100-125 Edsel discontinued, 1960	$50-75	$40-50	$30-40 Common	$30-40 Common
$100-125	$50-75	$40-50	$40-50	$40-50
$100-125	$50-75	$40-50	$40-50	$40-50
N.A.	N.A.	N.A.	N.A.	N.A.
$100-125	$50-75	$40-50	$40-50	$40-50
$100-125	$50-75	$40-50	$40-50	$40-50
$100-125	$50-75	$40-50	$40-50	$40-50
$175-200 Last DeSoto December 1960	N.A.	N.A.	N.A.	N.A.

Dealership lighters tend to be delightfully complicated, and are stunning if mint. This unused 1978 lighter has five colors. Despite its youth, it is very desirable. $80+

With six colors (black, red, white, brown, blue, and grey--be aware that the grey is very difficult to differentiate from the black in this photo), this 1972 lighter has almost everything. It is extremely detailed, has complicated and "politically incorrect" artwork, and is unused! $100+

This 1963 Ford logo is quite attractive. Four colors are present; but, compare this lighter with the previous two. Having the text in blue adds greatly to the overall attractiveness. $70+

With three or fewer colors, design complexity becomes more important. The 1964 Cummins lighter is mint and attractive, but less interesting than the '64 Cadillac/Olds dealership lighter, though each has three colors. *(A Zippo lighter from the same Cadillac dealership, but with a different logo, is in the Zippo Museum.)* Cadillac: $80+; Cummins: $50+

Both the uncommon green single color and the "busy" artwork make this full-stamp #2517191 lighter desirable. Compare with the six-color lighter. $60+

Basic black and block-letter text make this 1972 lighter an example of the least desirable advertising lighters. $35-40

A perfect 1953-55 Fisk Tire emblem lighter. A close look shows facial details, and a loupe will show the hand holding the lit candle. There is 100% enamel and 0% friction wear. With text on the back, this lighter is a real keeper—and one of my personal favorites. *(I never understood why a little boy would take a tire to bed, until I learned the Fisk Tire slogan: "Time to re-tire.")* $175+

This Chrysler master mechanic emblem lighter is every bit as mint as the previous, but has less detail and color. At first glance, the brass figure looks friction-worn, but the emblem originally came this way. These emblems were made for Chrysler for several years, though mint ones are uncommon. $130-150

A 1956 Lycoming emblem. The engine is extremely detailed and, although this lighter is used, there is only very slight rub wear to the engine where the brass has a reddish hue. The green inlay also shows minor flaking and cracking. $90-110

Cadillac emblem. This emblem, at best, was small and plain—and now there is corrosion that detracts greatly from the original appeal. The difference in desirability between this lighter and the next one is certainly debatable. $30-35

A Casite emblem on a three-barrel lighter. Attractive and clean, there are signs of minor friction wear, most notably in the yellow areas. Note the tiny ring around the emblem, indicative of originality on an emblem lighter. $130-150

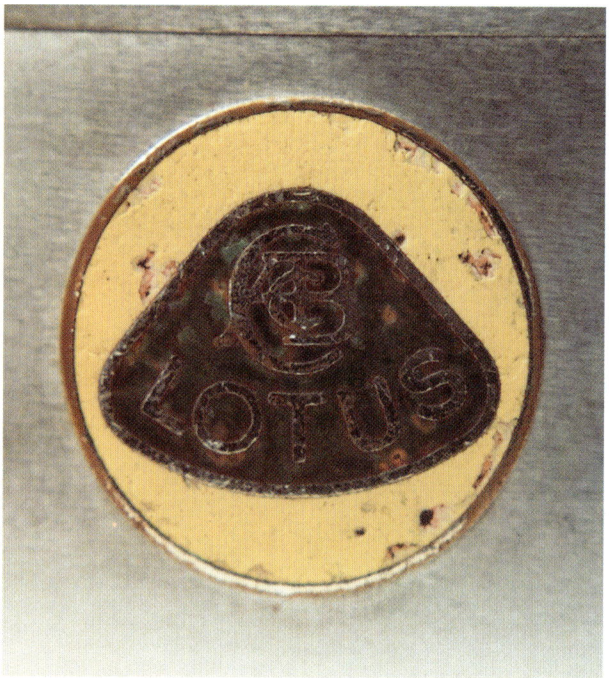

A 1971 Lotus lighter. Note the chipping, cracking and paint loss on the large emblem. This emblem is as big around as a quarter, magnifying relatively minor flaws. A mint example would be beautiful. $30-35.

This example has slight wear to the body of the case and the top of the lid. This might be called five percent brassing at most, but even five percent has a huge effect on values, and repainting any brassed-through lighter looks odd, at best. This lighter retains perhaps 25% of its paint. $40-50

This Canadian lighter shows brassing around the entire edge, but retains most of its paint, and a tight, original hinge. The Canadian origin makes this lighter more valuable than its condition. $50-60

This lighter has a large brassed area on the lid and the right-hand *6*. Also, the chrome on the front of the lighter has worn almost completely through. The brass is visible through the chrome. $10-15

The brassing on this Nash lighter is less then 40%, but bad enough to ruin the rare lighter for all but "Nash-o-files." Even in this condition, though, it is rare. $50-60

This logo was once beautiful and colorful. Not anymore. About 40% brassing is enough to put this lighter almost at the bottom of the value "heap." It has also been re-hinged several times, as have most lighters in this condition. $15-20

The brassing on this lighter is almost 95%, an amazing amount of wear. It has also been re-hinged. Any of the lighters in this section would look ridiculous if repainted. Compare this lighter to the Dodge dealership lighter at the beginning of this section for an idea of what this must have looked like originally. $5-10

Automobile History

Automobile Beginnings

In 1769, a French artillery officer named Nicholas Joseph Cugnot built a three-wheeled steam-powered carriage of his own design, hoping it would run well enough to pull cannon. It *did* run...off the road, at about three miles an hour, and that was that. Cugnot and his fellows then got back on their horses and continued their regular job, which was annoying the British.

Cugnot's clunky contraption began the self-propelled era. Although the steam powered vehicle was used with impressive results in England (so successfully, that the railroad companies essentially harassed the huge steam omnibuses out of existence), the steam engine was more suited for locomotives than for individual cars as we know them now. So, the steam engine became successful...for trains. But for passenger cars, steam was essentially a dead end. The true future of small, efficient engines for passenger cars was in the internal combustion engine.

In 1860, a Belgian named Etienne Lenoir built a two-cycle internal combustion engine. It worked and was a commercial success, though not as a conveyance. He made a vehicle, and it ran, but there were no further developments, so Lenoir faded into history. A contemporary of Lenoir's, one Beau De Rochas, patented a four-cycle engine in 1862, but apparently never built one. The actual construction of the internal combustion engine was left to a German named Nicholas Otto, who built one in 1878. Then, in 1885, two fellows named Daimler and Benz independently built gasoline-powered conveyances that are considered the real ancestors of today's motorcar.

In the United States, there was much independent work on the internal combustion engine, but George Selden is, by default it seems, given credit for the invention of the four-cycle internal combustion engine. He filed a patent application in 1879 for the gasoline engine, a steering mechanism, and what was essentially a clutch. He didn't actually *build* his vehicle until much later, but for several years, every car maker had to pay Selden a royalty on his invention. All this flurry of independent worldwide activity laid the groundwork for what became the American automobile industry. There was a spirited battle between proponents of steam, electric, and gas conveyances, but the gasoline engine quickly became dominant.

Despite earlier experiments, the American auto industry is generally considered to have taken its first teetering steps in the last few years of the 1800s, when Duryea, Oldsmobile, Winton, and Pope began making vehicles. However, among the hordes of people involved in moving the car from idea to prototype to successful industry, two men stand out:

Two Rambler bicycle ads from 1892. Rambler became Jeffrey, which in turn became Nash. *All ad photos in this section are courtesy of Kristina Lynn Harris.*

William Crapo Durant, and Henry Ford. Each had such an effect on the auto industry that, without their respective contributions, the world landscape as we now it today, literally as well as figuratively, would be incomprehensibly different.

Billy Durant had an organizational vision unequaled in his day. In 1904, he bought the Buick Motor Car Company, intending to create a vast corporation making a variety of cars. A multi-make company could much more easily suffer reduced sales in a given line, as the other makes under the corporate aegis would make up for the shortfall. Durant wanted a well-rounded corporation, with several different divisions, each focusing on a particular task. (For many years, the General Motors slogan was, "A car for every purse and purpose.") Ironically, if not for Henry Ford, the corporation would have been very different.

Ford was one of the original companies intended for the GM family, but he insisted that Durant pay cash for his company. When Ransom Eli Olds heard of Ford's demands, he too insisted on a cash payment for his company, Reo. Durant and his partner, Benjamin Briscoe, couldn't raise enough hard cash, so the deal fell through, and Durant and Briscoe parted company.

Durant was determined, however. He tried again and, by 1908, the General Motors Corporation consisted of Buick, Cadillac, Oldsmobile, and Oakland (which essentially became Pontiac). Another irony is that, unable to obtain Reo, because of R.E. Old's insistence on cash, Durant acquired Oldsmobile, Old's former company. Reo built its last passenger car in 1936, while Oldsmobile is still very much in the car-building business.

Durant had a great vision, but wasn't terribly adept at the detailed day-to-day running of a large corporation. Due to some financial troubles caused by an all too rapid expansion, by 1910 Durant was removed from control of his company. Two men who would make their own names in the history of car making, Walter Chrysler and Charles Nash, replaced him.

In 1911, Durant, who could be said to have had the very unique hobby of founding car companies, created a new one. He joined forces with a Frenchman, who had some success in auto racing, by the name of Louis Chevrolet. Introduced in 1912, the Chevrolet was successful enough that by 1916, Durant, who had never lost hope of regaining charge of GM, was once more at the helm, when Chevrolet bought GM.

Durant had the fatal flaw of the industrial "Tragic Hero," however. He had great ideas, but he was neither very organized nor much of a manager. His re-arrival caused the frustrated departure of Charles

A 1912 Stevens-Duryea ad. Duryea was gone long before the Depression. Note the right-hand drive.

Nash, who bought the Jeffrey Company, and renamed it—wonder of wonders—Nash. He took Durant's idea of a multi-product corporation to Nash, and acquired Kelvinator refrigerators in 1936. The resulting company, Nash-Kelvinator Corporation, was always the best run and strongest of the independents, though not strong enough, as time would show.

Walter Chrysler couldn't handle Durant's mismanagement either and quit in 1920, as had Nash and Henry LeLand (who founded Cadillac and Lincoln) before him. Chrysler was looking for his own car company anyway, and found it in the financially troubled, yet still respected Maxwell Motor Car Company. In 1921, Maxwell was reorganized with Chrysler in charge, though he cleverly continued using the Maxwell name until the public had accepted his new Chrysler car. The Chrysler Corporation was then formed to take over Maxwell, and another child of Billy Durant was birthed. (Comedian Jack Benny, on his popular radio show, never spoke of any car but his Maxwell, which must have been a constant source of frustration to the advertising department at Chrysler.)

Early car ads. Maxwell became Chrysler and Autocar became a truck builder. The other companies are long gone.

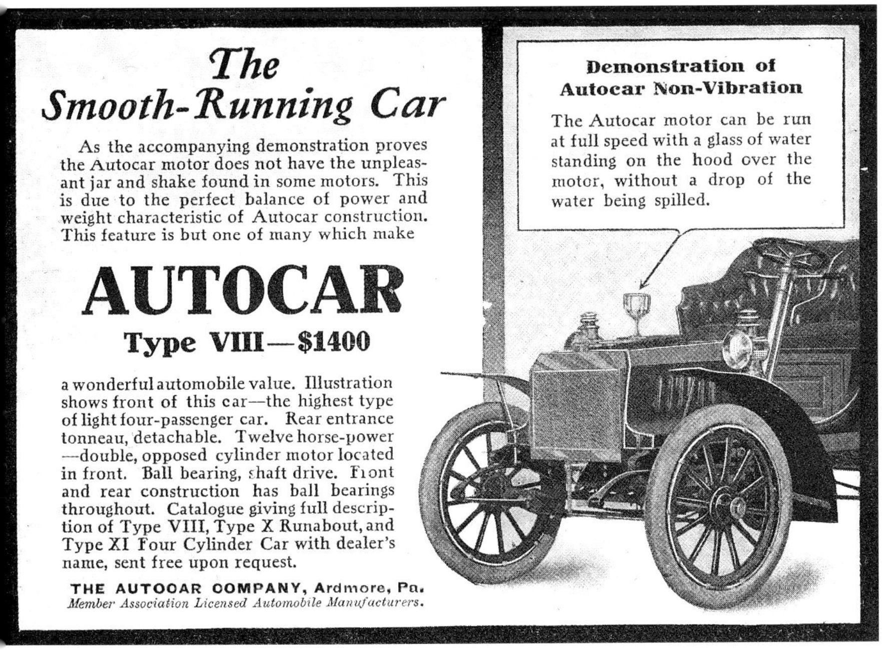

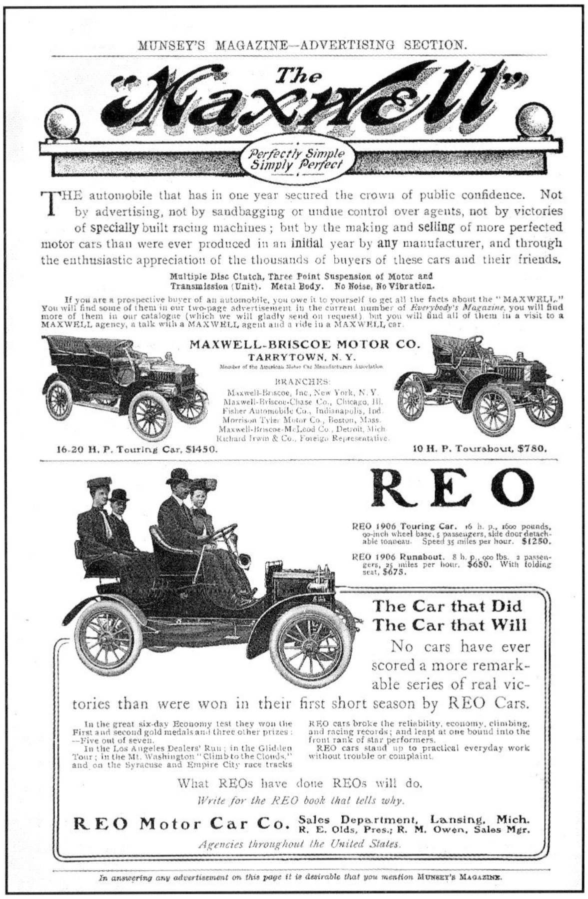

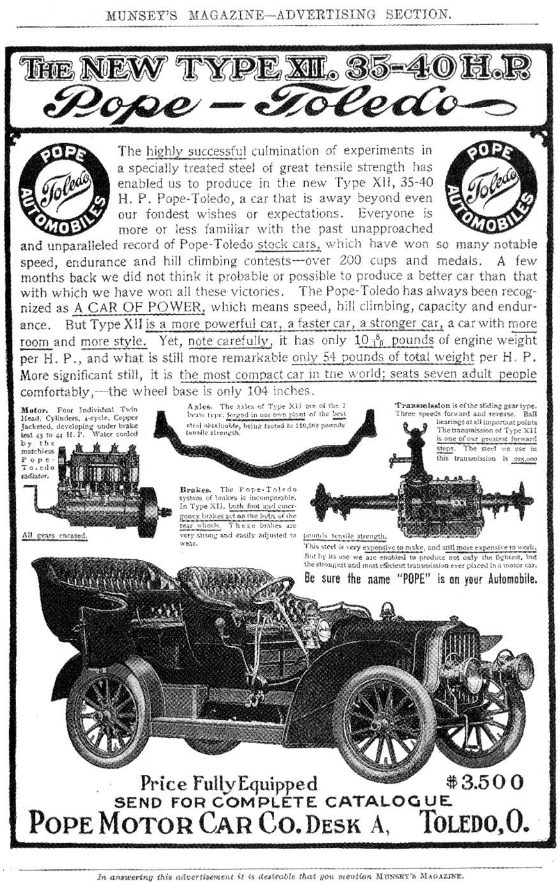

A Willys-Overland ad. Note the triumphant announcement of a price reduction to $750 for 1916. Meanwhile, in Ford country, an equivalent touring car sold for $360, down from $440 the previous year.

Another Willys ad. *This* ad mentions advances in technology, rather then price.

This 1925 Ford ad has a generic text, making claims that could be made of any car. The prices, however, are uniquely Ford's. The way to beat Ford was with innovation, and not price.

A 1925 Chevrolet ad. General Motors pioneered innovative ways to purchase cars. Note the price in the ad, higher then that of an equivalent Ford.

Like Nash, Chrysler believed in the multi-layer corporation, but he took it much farther. In 1928, he bought the Dodge Brothers Manufacturing Company, and introduced DeSoto and Plymouth. The resulting company was the third member of what became the "big three," and continues today, although the DeSoto division was quietly killed off in late 1960.

The year 1920 also saw the second departure of Durant from GM, when GM was—again—in severe financial troubles. Pierre Du Pont took on the company debts in exchange for control and Durant's resignation. The company's condition was so severe that there was talk of discontinuing Chevrolet—an amazing thought today, when Chevrolet makes a million-plus cars a year.

Durant wasn't quite finished, however. He amassed seven million dollars in loans and started another company, Durant Motors, intending to do again what he had done with General Motors. Unfortunately, Durant Motors succumbed to the Depression in 1933. Billy Durant declared bankruptcy in 1935, reduced, literally, to sweeping floors in bowling alleys. He died in 1947.

Billy Durant had the ability to see the need for not just a car company making a single-line of vehicles, but also for several car companies, sharing parts, research and labor. It is quite surprising that no other company saw such a need at that time. Almost every company—including Ford—was a single line manufacturer, and most of them died as single line manufacturers. Others merged, too late to save themselves, and died as multi-make corporations. General Motors, on the other hand, became, by the mid-1930s, the largest corporation in the world, and the largest privately owned company the world has ever seen. If Durant was the Prophet, it remained for his disciples to perfect the dream. Chrysler, Nash, and Durant's own successor, Alfred Sloan, had skills he lacked; but, the original vision was William Durant's, and for that he will be remembered as long as there is a General Motors Corporation.

Any list of automotive giants must begin with Henry Ford, who dreamed of—and made—"a car for the great multitude." He is most responsible for taking the "wealthy plaything" and making it truly available to the common man. In doing so, he became such a folk hero in the minds of the "American Public" that his many negative traits were overlooked. He was involved in the creation or rescue of several car companies, including Cadillac, Lincoln, Mercury, and—very unwillingly—Dodge.

Henry Ford's contribution to American industry was the adaptation of the moving assembly line to car making. The assembly line wasn't new, but Ford's treatment of it was, and by 1914, the entire chassis of the Model T could be built in about ninety minutes. The resulting savings in labor costs allowed the price of a Ford to reach as low as $290, placing car ownership within the reach of almost every American. In 1916, Ford made over half a million cars, and the U.S.A. was truly on wheels.

An interesting and unintended consequence of the emergence of the practical and affordable Ford was found in its unsettling impact upon the populace of the Soviet Union. When John Steinbeck's *Grapes Of Wrath* came out as a 1940 movie starring Henry Fonda, the Soviets pounced on it as an example of how horribly the American worker suffered at the hands of the capitalists. After about six weeks of being shown all over the U.S.S.R., however, the movie was pulled from all theaters. Some brave soul had pointed out that despite their sufferings, the Joads had a car, and nobody, but *nobody*, in the U.S.S.R. had a car, or any hope of ever having one. (Stalin probably had him shot, and most of the film industry too, for good measure.) Ford made that possible, and the achievement was enough to ensure him a place in American history. Other aspects of Henry Ford were less favorable, however.

He is famous for announcing that he would pay workers five dollars a day, simultaneous with the creation of the assembly line. That was about twice the going wage paid to Detroit autoworkers at the time. Although Ford ordered fire hoses turned on the immense throngs of men who applied for employment, he was again hailed as a hero of the common man. Those who sought that wage had to meet some grim requirements, however.

Working six months before being eligible for that wage wasn't unusual; but workers had to be "worthy" of it, as well. That meant they had to live according to the beliefs of Henry Ford, and Ford organized a "Sociological Department" to monitor the private lives of employees. Ford's real goal was simple and astonishing. He was one of the most active anti-Semites industrialized America has ever seen, and he wanted to make very sure he had none working for him. He also hated Communists and his—literally—violent opposition to unionization of his employees was largely because he thought that the communists were behind the efforts to organize labor. (There was indeed a communist faction in the early union movement, but not to the extent that Ford believed.) The result was that Ford was the last car company to negotiate with what became the UAW, and it didn't happen until 1941.

Henry Ford was phenomenally efficient in the way he ran his company. He bought whole forests so he could supply his own wood, required in the car bodies of the day. He took scrap wood, charred it, and pressed it into charcoal briquettes. Unhappy with the quality of the glass in his cars, he created a new glass making process, and bought a glass company in 1923. Next to this obvious brilliance, his many odd traits stagger the mind of one who knows only of the industrial genius.

Ford was famous for being hard to work for, or with, and he had fights with many of the other early auto pioneers, including two with Henry LeLand. Ford's daughter-in-law, Eleanor, swore that he drove his son, Edsel Ford, to an early grave. And he was stubbornly resistant to any kind of change in his vehicles. In 1912, after only a few years on the market, Ford's engineering staff felt the need for an improved Model T. While Ford and his wife were on vacation, the staff designed and built a prototype of the more advanced vehicle. When Ford returned from vacation to see what had occurred in his absence, he went mad with rage and destroyed the prototype with his bare hands. In 1926, an executive who wrote a tactful—*very* tactful, given that he certainly remembered the events of 1912—memo about the need to replace the Model T was fired.

The Model T wasn't an advanced car, even for the time. Early examples had no fuel pump, for instance, relying instead on gravity to move gas to the engine. Therefore, they had to be driven backwards up even moderate inclines. Many other car companies had electric starters long before Ford offered one in 1919—as an extra-cost option. On the other hand, the "flivver" was simple, easy to drive and repair, powerful for the time, and cheap. Above all, that car was *cheap*—to build, buy, and operate. In short, it was the perfect product for the dawning of an industry. So the Model T was built until 1927, not because it remained—or ever had been—a state-of-the-art car, but because Ford didn't want to change it.

Other car companies, including Dodge, Essex, Chevrolet, Ajax, Star (Durant's low-price car) and Viking (Oldsmobile's low-end companion), introduced more advanced low-priced vehicles that slowly lowered Ford's market share. There was also competition from Ford's own Model T's, which saturated the used-car market with cars not much different from those still rolling off the assembly lines. The Model A, then, was a response forced from Ford by other companies. Introduced in 1928, it was successful enough to retake the market share Ford had lost, but was an example of an intractability that caused Ford Motors many problems until well after Ford's death in 1947.

Therefore, by the time George Blaisdell introduced his cigarette lighter in 1933, the auto industry had become a two-tiered list of companies; the big three, who exist today essentially as they did in 1933 (though a whole lot bigger) and everyone else. Under the heading of "everyone else" were companies that made fine cars, but doomed, every one, to be outlasted by the big boys of auto-making ... and by Blaisdell's little Zippo lighter, two inches by two ounces of wind-proof flame.

The Independents and the Depression

From the beginning of the 20th century, when anyone with a machine shop and a bit of ingenuity could start a car company, to the turn of the 21st century, when the total number of car companies world-wide is around a dozen, is a story that an entire library could not adequately tell. Much of the "shrinkage" occurred during the recession after World War One. But another epidemic was to come. It started in October of 1929, just as the new model year cars were hitting showrooms. Six months later, most of those cars were still sitting on showroom floors, as the Great Depression set in for a prolonged and unpleasant visit.

Quotable Comments

"Cars can be made so that without animals they will move with unbelievable rapidity."

Roger Bacon, writing in the 13th century.

"If you dislike my car, go and build yourself a better one."

Alexander Winton, to James Packard. Packard bought a Winton car and was unhappy enough with it to journey to Cleveland from Warren, Ohio, to complain. Packard accepted Winton's challenge and did, indeed, make " a better car."

"You can't get people to sit over an explosion."

Albert Pope, explaining to Hiram Maxim why he was going to eschew gas engines and concentrate on electric vehicles. Maxim was the son of the inventor of the Maxim Gun, one of the first workable machine guns, so the occasional explosion probably didn't put him off.

"All the gasoline engines we have seen belch forth from their exhaust pipe continuous streams of thick smoke with a highly noxious odor. Imagine thousands of such vehicles on the streets, each offering up its column of smell!"

Engineer Pedro Salom, writing in 1896 of the evils of the gasoline engine. He probably forgot to add that he himself was producing an electric vehicle, the Electrobat, at the time.

"To me, the gasoline automobile is a clumsy, dangerous, noisy brute of a vehicle. They're going to catch fire, they're not safe, they blow up, accidents will happen, a lot of people are going to be killed. The damn things stink to high heaven, they shake your liver to pieces, they always break down at the worst moment, and in short they are a public nuisance and even worse, a public menace!"

John M. Studebaker, tactfully rendering his opinion of the gasoline powered car. Immediately after this pronouncement, gasoline cars appeared alongside Studebaker's beloved electrics. (*Car & Parts,* December 1997, 60)

(Unless otherwise noted, quotes from Rae 1965)

"Possession of a motorcar is such an ostentatious display of wealth that it will stimulate Socialism by inciting envy of the rich."

Woodrow Wilson in 1906. The Model T was introduced in 1908, and the resulting envy came from the rest of the world.

"The general use of automobiles will relieve traffic congestion."

The Automobile Magazine*, in 1909.*

"Just think of all the Ford owners who will someday want an automobile!"

John Dodge, when asked why he and his brother were going to make cars themselves, cutting ties to Ford, for whom they had supplied components. The relationship between the Dodges and Ford was turbulent, and they did not part friends. The early Dodge Brothers logo included a Star of David, allegedly to annoy the violently anti-Semitic Ford. (Car & Parts, August 1998, 56)

"America is the only country in the world where you can go to the poor house in an automobile!"

Will Rogers, at the height of the Depression.

"I've got no use for an engine that has more cylinders then a cow has teats."

Henry Ford, stubbornly refusing to move up from a 4 to a 6-cylinder engine. He eventually skipped to an 8-cylinder, the first low-priced V-8 ever. (Car & Parts, June 1997, 62*)*

"The hurtful thing is that Father takes Harry' s word, and he won't believe mine!"

A grieving Edsel Ford, to his wife. Harry Bennet was a thug, and Edsel Ford loathed him (as did almost everyone else in the Ford employ) but he was Henry's right-hand man, and the elder Ford seemed to make it clear on many occasions that Bennet's counsel and trust were more important to him than his own son's. (Car & Parts, June 1997, 64*)*

"If future merger on any scale is going to be necessary, merger NOW while companies are strong would be the soundest course."

George Romney, then Vice President of Nash and eventually head of American Motors, writing in 1948. His advice was good. It was not heeded. (Foster 1993)

Two 1933 Packard ads. Packards were nothing if not beautiful. Note the slogan; "Ask the woman who owns one."

In 1935, when advertising first appeared on Zippo lighters, car makers were coming out of the world of the Great Depression with much relieved brow mopping at having survived the darkest economic period in American history. There was much cause for relief, as many companies had already succumbed, though others would fade into history by the end of the decade.

American Austin was born in 1930 as an Americanized version of the British Austin and died by 1934, after making some tiny cars that can only be described as "darling." Reborn in 1937 as American Bantam, it would survive only long enough to compete in the military trials for the vehicle that became the Jeep.

Auburn was dying in 1935, though it lived long enough to produce the supercharged 851/852 Speedster, one of the most beautiful—and valuable—cars ever built. Cord ceased making cars in 1932, but returned in 1936. The Cord models 810 and 812 are treasures today, but legal problems forced Errett Lobban Cord to cease all production in 1937. Duesenberg was also a child of E. L. Cord, and it too went out of business in 1937, if having made fewer than 500 cars over the previous decade can be called being *in* business.

Billy Durant's last child, Durant Motors, died in 1933. Franklin, famous for its air-cooled engines, folded in 1934.

Graham and Hupmobile survived the Depression. Research has not turned up a Zippo lighter touting either of these car companies, but a verifiable one would be very desirable. The cars they made are

A 1933 Lincoln ad. Luxury car makers made their ads as lavish as possible, even during the Depression. Note the Lincoln's price.

LaSalle, Cadillac's low-price companion make.

Black & white ads are more typical of the lower-end cars like Chevrolet.

desirable as well, and equally scarce. Each company stopped selling cars before W.W.II, though Graham actually built the first Frasers.

Marmon is a name few outside the car hobby remember, though Marmons were excellent cars with a loyal following since 1905. The 700 plus cars made in 1932, however, were the last. Pierce-Arrow was gone in 1936, and 1936 also saw the final Reo passenger cars, although Reo and Diamond-Reo continued making trucks before being bought by truck giant White. Stutz made fewer then 1,500 cars between 1930-35, and was gone by the time Zippo lighters began trumpeting Kendall's 2000-mile oil.

The makers listed here are actually the fortunate ones, because history remembers them. The Automobile Manufacturer's Association and the Automobile Club of Michigan compiled a list of over three thousand car makes, made by over fifteen hundred distinct manufacturers. Those vehicles are not even remembered, consigned to the scrap drives of W.W.II without a single example remaining to show that they ever existed. It is indicative of the aura of the American automobile that this fact is regretful to many.

What They Did Before They Made Cars

Hudson ran a department store in Detroit. It still exists.

Rambler, Winton, Willys and Pope made Bicycles (and Pope kept making bicycles.)

Pierce-Arrow made, of all things, bird cages.

Marmon made flour-milling machinery.

Henry Leland, founder of both Cadillac and Lincoln (named for the first man he had voted for, in 1864) was a New England gun maker.

Maxwell-Briscoe (later Chrysler) made sheet metal.

Studebaker and Durant made carriages and wagons. (This *was* a long time ago.)

White made sewing machines.

Peerless made clothes wringers....*clothes wringers*?

Crosley made radios.

Buick made plumbing supplies.

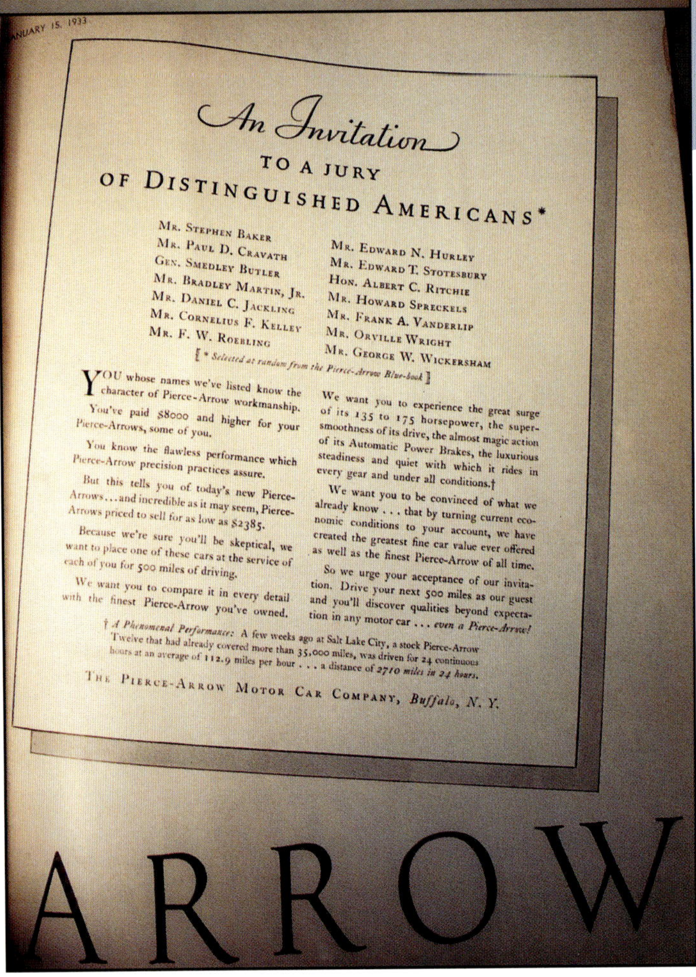

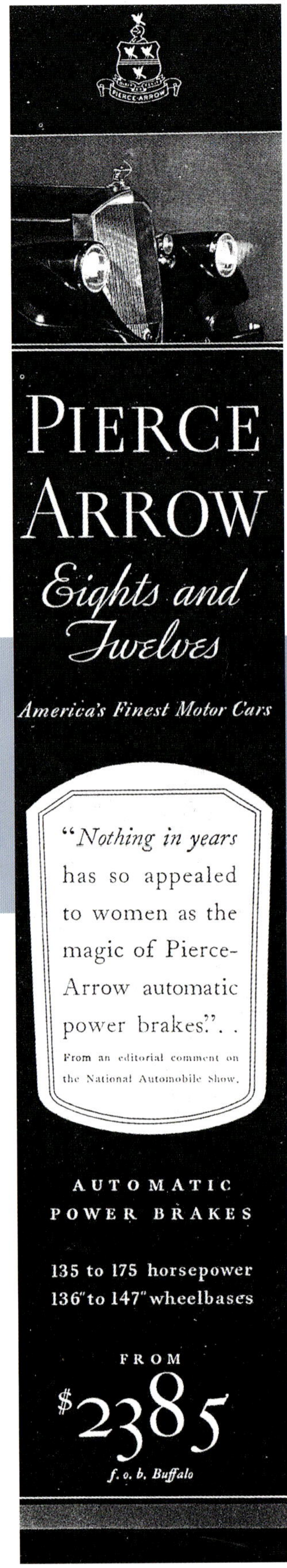

Pierce-Arrow was struggling, and these black & white ads are typical. Owners included Orville Wright.

Beautiful Cadillac ads from 1933.

Nash was a well-run company, and usually could afford ads as nice as this one from 1933.

The bottom text of this 1933 Buick ad is unfortunately worded. Note the script Buick logo.

A typical war-time Zippo lighter ad. Zippo lighters remained in production throughout the war, though with inferior steel, which was painted black and then baked.

ZIPPO to the rescue

ZIPPO is in the War!

Zippo Windproof LIGHTERS have acted as rescue beacons for men in open boats, as a guide through dense dark jungles and as a means of lighting fires for food and warmth. Lighting lanterns as well as pipes is a regular duty for a ZIPPO. Its water-tight case is a life saver.

So, if you are in the service and are going "over there", where matches are scarce and sometimes difficult to light, you'll be glad to have Zippo, the world's most practical windproof lighter, and the choice of the men in the Service.

We now can furnish ZIPPO Windproof LIGHTERS only to our Armed Forces outside of continental United States, and to post exchanges at ports of embarkation and ship service stores on board ship. We hope your local dealer can still supply you — the factory consumer stock is done and gone until metals essential for victory are again available. Sorry.

ZIPPO MANUFACTURING CO., 7 Barbour St., BRADFORD, PA., New York Office: 52 Vanderbilt Ave.

Windproof, water-tight, permanent wick, hard flint, large fuel capacity, always dependable — that's ZIPPO.

FOR VICTORY BUY

Invest that $2.50, for the ZIPPO you may not be able to buy, in WAR STAMPS till the days of peace arrive.

FOR YOUR PROTECTION *Look for this engraving* ZIPPO PAT. 2032695 MADE IN U.S.A. *on the bottom of every genuine* ZIPPO LIGHTER

ZIPPO *Windproof* **LIGHTER**

The Post-War Years

During W.W.II, the United States' economy was geared wholly towards the war effort. The shift towards war production began even before the attack on Pearl Harbor. It was generally thought that the U.S. would eventually be drawn into the conflagration that had begun in September 1939 with Hitler's invasion of Poland.

Domestic car production slowed drastically as steel, rubber, and other war materials became harder to obtain, and finally stopped completely between February 1942 and August 1945. When car production began again, the vehicles were, of necessity, hardly changed from the immediate pre-war years, but no one cared. Anything that would drive was salable, and it all sold. Every company still in business sold all the cars it made, and each could easily have sold twice as many. The returning GI wanted nothing more than to return to his life and family, buy a new car and forget the horrific years spent fighting. One thing wasn't forgotten, however; the Zippo lighter he had carried.

Unlike most American companies, which turned from their usual products to making war material, Zippo lighters were produced during the war; but, all production went to military Post Exchanges, for sale only to members of the Armed Forces. George Blaisdell, ever the salesman, sent many Zippo lighters to military leaders during the war and made them available to servicemen in every theater of war. (Immortal war correspondent Ernie Pyle even waxed poetic about the Zippo lighter in one of his articles.) The combination of salesmanship, quality of product, and genuine kindness shown to soldiers throughout the war created a sense of goodwill that still exists today.

Zippo lighter sales exploded because the war had proven the little lighter's reliability—as well as the company's integrity—in the most extreme circumstances. When a soldier returned home, his wartime Zippo lighter was usually retired to souvenir duty and replaced with a new one—and not just one, either.

Men and women bought Zippo lighters for "work or play," and fancier models for special events. An evening at the theater or opera called for an ornate

Above and center: A used "black crackle" Zippo lighter from W.W.II. The three-barrel hinge on this one indicates a date of 1943 or later. Note the rounded bottom. There is a sharp price difference between the four and three-barrel hinge black crackles. Though slightly used, this lighter is in excellent original condition. $300-350

Right: This ad, on display in the Zippo Museum, was very accurate. *Everybody* bought new Zippo lighters.

BUICK

CADILLAC

CROSLEY

Drive It Away!

Your first look at 1941's cars will give you an impression of massiveness; of sleek, close-to-the-ground length. You'll see 1941's characteristic lines in more models than ever before, with builders generally expanding into wider price-and-model ranges.

Bodies are even wider than last year's, with fenders, lamps and bumpers often streamlined into them. Vision has been increased. Running boards may be standard, concealed, or absent altogether. Brighter colors predominate, with increased use of two-tone combinations, while interiors are going luxuriously modern.

Many of this year's cars have increased horsepower and higher compression ratios and lower operating costs. You'll like the further simplification of driving through improved transmissions and wider use of the liquid-drive principle. New gadgets are: electrically operated tops on open jobs, windows that flip up or down at a button-touch, electrical direction signals. In short, here's your new car.

PHOTOGRAPHED FOR COLLIER'S BY VALENTINO SARRA

FORD

MERCURY 8

NASH

PLYMOUTH

PONTIAC

VROLET

CHRYSLER

SOTO

DODGE

DSON

LINCOLN-ZEPHYR

SMOBILE

PACKARD

DEBAKER

WILLYS

Previous two pages: This photograph, from a 1940 *Collier's*, shows all the car companies still in business at the start of the 1941 model year. Graham, Hupmobile, Terraplane, Lafayette, and LaSalle are gone.

This page: Two sets of car lighters, commemorating the decades after W.W.II. Full sets in the original package are rare. Sets are worth $125-150 complete.

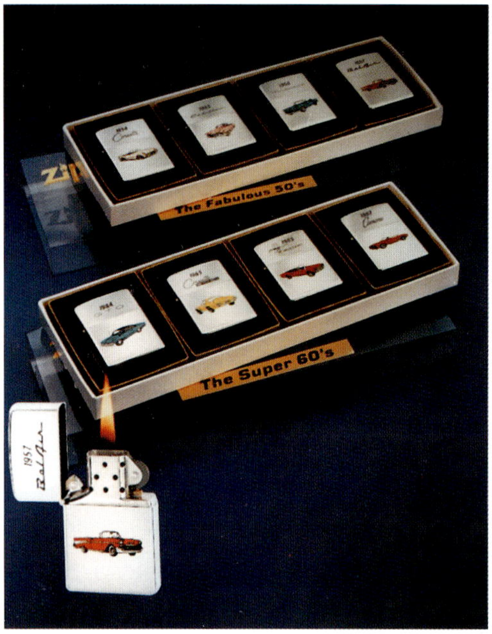

Zippo lighter commensurate with the occasion. Even non-smoking men carried them, hoping to be the gallant knight and provide a light for some "matchless" girl. The Zippo lighter became a part of many men's and women's daily equipment. Advertisers took note, and *everybody*, even such groups as the Salvation Army, ordered lighters with their logos on them. Business was booming in Bradford, as well as in Detroit. Almost every major car company advertised on a Zippo after W.W.II. (Crosley is surprisingly absent, with not a single piece of artwork in the Zippo archives.)

After the war, stock fraud was a common moneymaking scam. Knowing that everyone had money, wanted cars, and would buy anything on wheels, several "fake" car companies were created. The usual ploy was to actually build a few vehicles with some gimmick and show them at car shows around the U.S. Then, stock was sold in the new company, which would promptly fold. Among these "fake" car companies were Playboy and Davis, the latter creating a three-wheeled affair that saw seventeen copies made. No examples of Playboy or Davis artwork were found in the Zippo files, although it is amusing to think that, with a minimum order of twenty-five units, any lighters produced would actually outnumber the cars made by the company. Tucker was covered by the same cloud, but was exonerated (see the Tucker section).

If the Depression began the demise of the American independent car maker, then the battle between Ford and Chevrolet in the 1950s finished the job. In 1953, Henry Ford II decided to make Ford the nation's number one car maker again, "or break it in the process." He began shipping record numbers of cars to dealers, whether they had been ordered or not. Ford dealers were not happy. The glut of cars forced Ford dealers to discount heavily. This resulted, of course, in lots of new Fords being sold. Chevy followed suit, with similar results; lots of unhappy Chevrolet dealers, lots of new, massively discounted Chevys. Customers were happy.

There was much worried hand wringing from the independents, however, and a paucity of new Hudsons, Nashs or Studebakers. Even in a banner year, the independent car makers produced only a fraction of the cars manufactured by the "big three." Because a loss in one area could not be offset by profits in another, independent dealers were unable to discount cars to match Ford or Chevrolet. For instance, in 1946, Hudson had 27 million dollars in the bank. That seems like a whole lot of money, but Chevrolet budgeted four times that amount just to build a bigger plant. In 1954, Chevrolet made 1.4

million cars. All the independents *combined* made a mere 221,730, just about one sixth of the production by that single division of General Motors. Chevy and Ford could afford razor-thin profits—or even losses—on their cars, whereas the smaller companies could not. So the independents remained unhappy, but not for too much longer. The landscape had changed forever.

Perhaps it is unfair to blame the demise of the American independent on Ford, because the result was inevitable, and had been since the formation of General Motors. Big boys get bigger; small boys become plumbers. The Ford-Chevy war merely sped up the process a bit.

Even Chrysler was weakened so severely that some wags began referring to "the Big Two-and-a-Half." The stodgy styling and under-powered engines of the post-war Chryslers didn't help. Chrysler was forced to borrow $100 million to re-tool. This resulted in some of the most beautiful Chryslers ever made, powered by the amazing 'hemi" engine. With four different divisions, Chrysler was able to weather the Chevy-Ford storm, although it would not really be healthy again until the mid-1960s, and DeSoto was eliminated altogether in late 1960. Regardless, by the beginning of the 1955 model year, Ford had not caught Chevrolet.

However, Henry Ford II's gambit had essentially killed the independent car maker. Merger and demise was the order of the day. Kaiser joined with Willys-Overland, Packard bought Studebaker, and Nash merged with Hudson to form American Motors. Little Crosley faded away in 1952 (although President Eisenhower used one as a golf cart for a time).

The problem was that the merging companies, even the well-run Nash, were weak, and two weak partners do not make one strong one. The advantages that blessed Chrysler and Durant were not present when the independents joined forces.

Although all the proud names were—for the moment—still present, the independent car companies had shrunk to just three. Packard cars used Studebaker bodies in 1957-58, Hudsons became Nashes with Hudson nameplates, and Kaiser-Willys stopped making passenger cars completely in the United States. Kaiser moved to South America and made cars in Argentina until 1962. Only the indomitable Jeep continued to be sold in the U.S., by Kaiser-Jeep. Of all the American companies in this book outside the "big three," only Jeep remains in the passenger car pantheon as a division of Daimler-Chrysler. One of the great ironies of the American automobile is that Jeep is now owned by those whom it was created to fight against.

The lighters illustrated in the next section are almost all post-war lighters, and they represent only a tiny fraction of the vast array manufactured over the years since 1945. Not even Zippo management knows how many different types of artwork went on Zippo lighters. This lack of information creates another mystery: how many? We'll never know, but it sure is fun to try to find out.

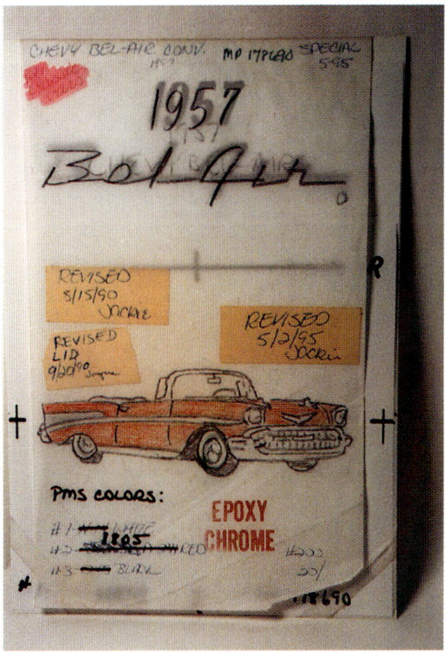

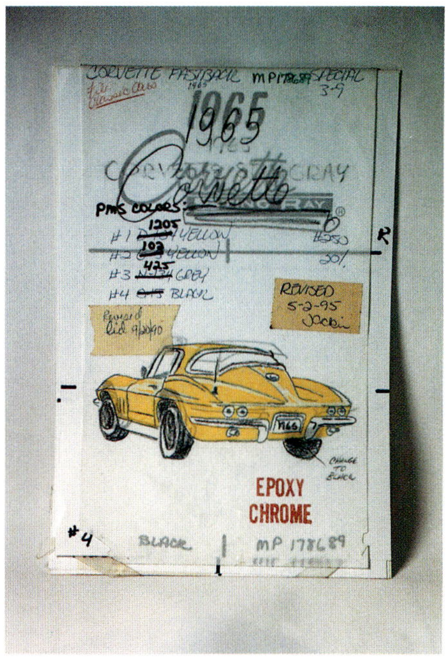

Some of the artwork for the series lighters.

The Zippo Car

Sometime in 1947, George Blaisdell took a walk next door from Zippo Manufacturing to the Bauschard Chrysler dealership. There he made arrangements to buy a 1947 Chrysler Saratoga for $2048. Blaisdell then had the car shipped to Gardner Displays in Pittsburgh, where, for a whopping 25 thousand dollars, it became the Zippo Car.

The body of the car was fitted with two huge Zippo lighters. When open, the chimneys were toped with plastic flames that duplicated the ones in Zippo lighter ads. When not in use, the flames were stored in the trunk, and the lids of the giant lighters snapped shut.

The Zippo Car was a popular parade car during its brief life. However, the Chrysler chassis was inadequate to handle the car's greatly increased weight. The result was a basically unsatisfactory vehicle with frequently blown tires. An attempt to modify the original Zippo Car was unsuccessful and, during the attempt, the car was disassembled and the various parts were lost.

Although the original Zippo Car disappeared, along with the original blueprints, a second was built in 1997, based on a 1947 Chrysler New Yorker. For the second iteration, the suspension was strengthened to handle the additional weight, and the electrical system was upgraded to accommodate air conditioning.

The Zippo Car appeared on a run of Zippo lighters in 1948, and the commemorative lighter in 1998 also honored the Zippo Car. Original 1948 Zippo Car lighters are very valuable and the Limited Edition 1998 lighter promises to be a "keeper" as time goes on.

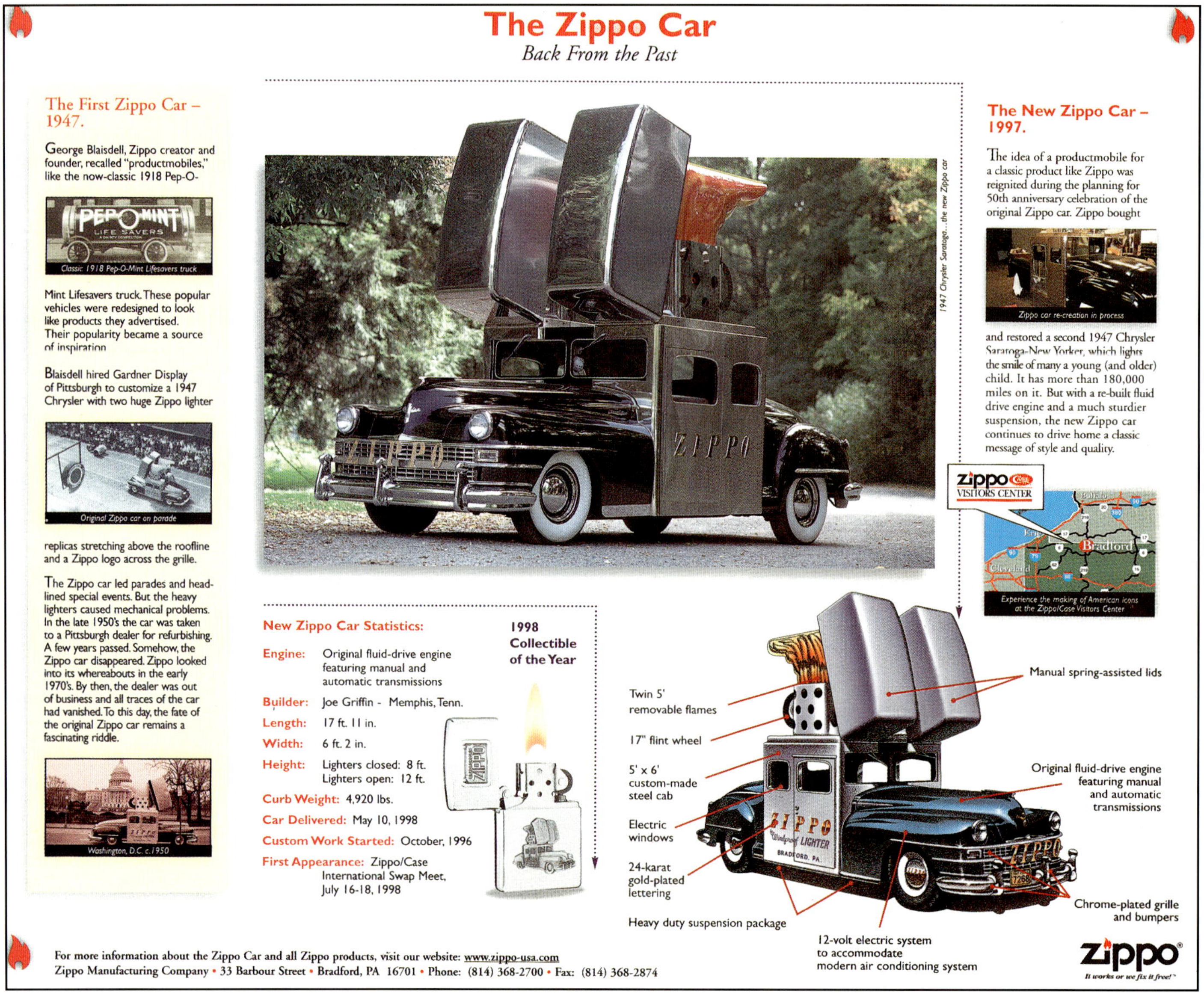

A Zippo Manufacturing poster about the Zippo cars, old and new.

An original photo of the Zippo car.

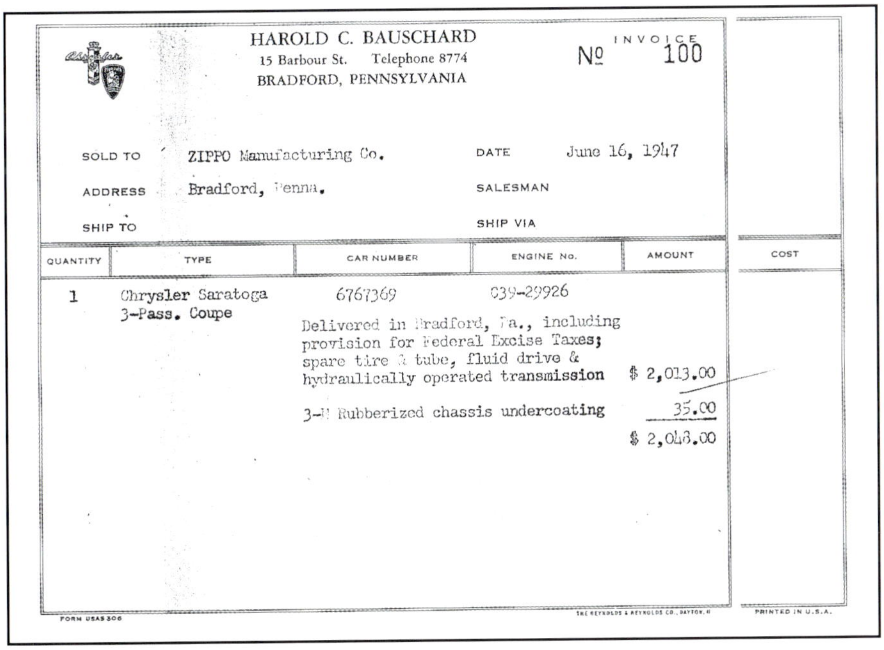

HAROLD C. BAUSCHARD
15 Barbour St. Telephone 8774
BRADFORD, PENNSYLVANIA

INVOICE № 100

SOLD TO ZIPPO Manufacturing Co. DATE June 16, 1947
ADDRESS Bradford, Penna. SALESMAN
SHIP TO SHIP VIA

QUANTITY	TYPE	CAR NUMBER	ENGINE No.	AMOUNT	COST
1	Chrysler Saratoga 3-Pass. Coupe	6767369	039-29926		
		Delivered in Bradford, Pa., including provision for Federal Excise Taxes; spare tire & tube, fluid drive & hydraulically operated transmission		$ 2,013.00	
		3-M Rubberized chassis undercoating		35.00	
				$ 2,048.00	

FORM USAS 306 THE REYNOLDS & REYNOLDS CO., DAYTON, O PRINTED IN U.S.A.

This is the original invoice for the first Zippo Car. It has never before been published.

An original Zippo car Zippo lighter. *Courtesy Zippo Mfg.* $800+

Cars & Cardboards

This section contains all the automotive "cardboards" currently in the archives of Zippo Manufacturing. Each "cardboard" shows a design or logo that was actually produced. Every bit of artwork here, *unless it has "Do not use"* or *"restricted"* written on it, appeared on at least twenty-five Zippo Lighters. Most of the illustrated cardboards have dates on them, which make it possible to almost exactly date a given lighter. Comparing a cardboard's date to a bottom stamp on a lighter will help clear up much of the confusion about pre-date code stamps.

Many "cardboards" have been lost over the years, and what is illustrated here is literally only a tiny fraction of the automotive artwork used on Zippo Lighters. Most of the lighters illustrated in this book do not have the corresponding "cardboard" they were made from. Interestingly, actual cars on car company lighters are rare, yet cars on lighters advertising other products are fairly common. The explanation for this is simple.

Car lighters were ordered in—usually—rather large lots. Even an individual dealer would almost always order more than twenty-five lighters. To put a specific vehicle on a lighter incurred the risk that the next year's model would be different enough to render any remaining lighters obsolete. A company' s logo, however, remained the same, and lighters would still be useable the next season. Also, newly introduced car *names*, like the Olds 88, Nash Airflyte, ("Airflyte" was the name for the entire 1948 Nash lineup of cars) are fairly common on lighters.

On the other hand, highly detailed renderings of specific vehicles on lighters advertising other products are fairly common. A 1953 Jeep, for example, on a group of lighters advertising a refrigerator company was still useable in '54.

Car Names We'll Never See Again

Confederate- Chevrolet
Rebel-Rambler
Wasp-Hudson
Dictator-Studebaker
La Femme- Dodge

This mint lighter shows a Ford vehicle, possibly a Mercury Cougar or a Lincoln Continental. Note the price tag still on the lighter. $40-50

This is a "surrey" version of the famous Jeep, an arrangement once popular at resort hotels. *Courtesy Ed Pinedo.* $30-40

A Canadian four-color Zippo lighter with an advertisement for an ambulance company. The tail fins and windshield design make this an early 1960s Cadillac. Note the paint loss—although it is still a great piece. $50-60

A 1956 cardboard for a funeral home. The Cadillac is very recognizable.

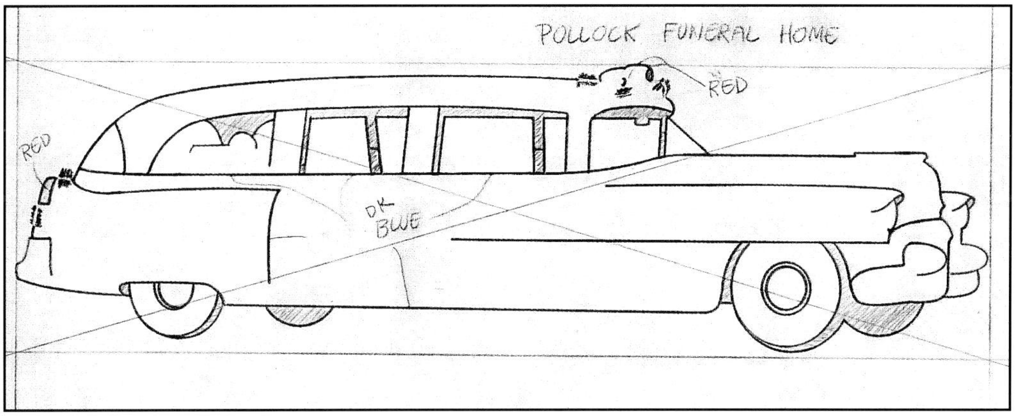

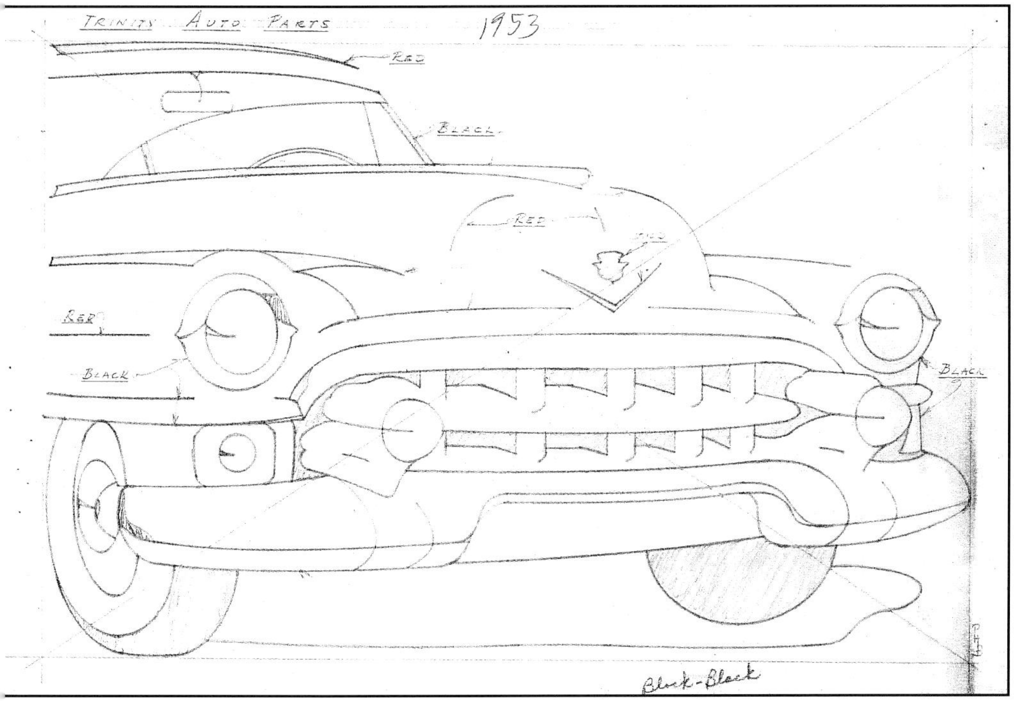

A Cadillac on a 1953 cardboard advertising an auto parts store. The detail is marvelous.

A wonderfully detailed 1953 cardboard, showing a Willys Jeep. The color combination is unusual.

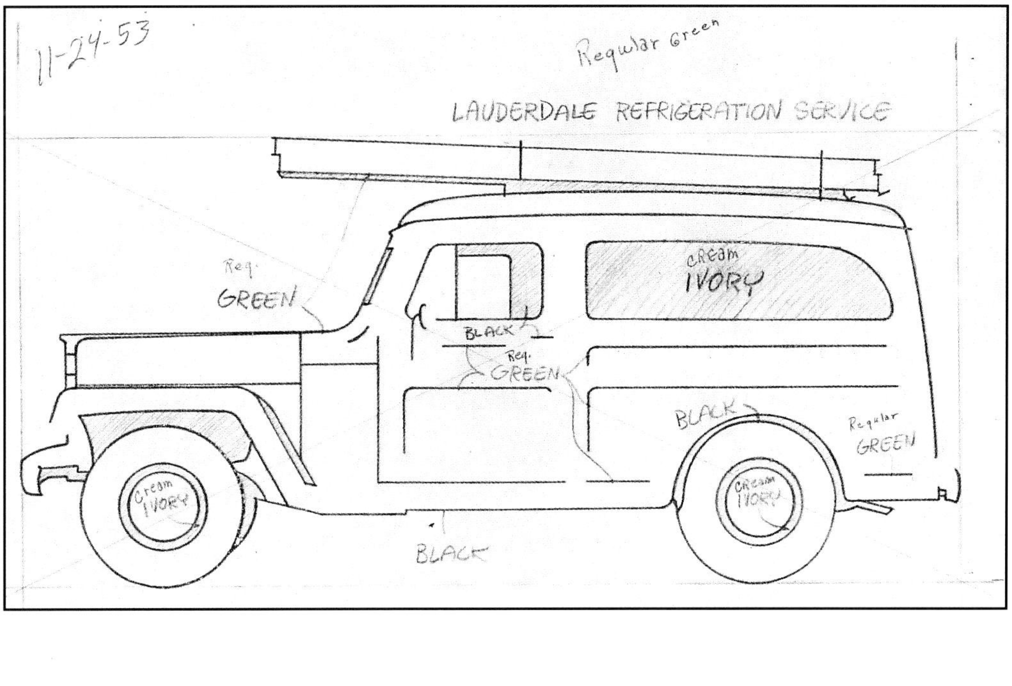

The Independents

American Motors

Nash

The story of Nash is an amazing example of the opportunities available to people of ingenuity and dedication at the beginning of the twentieth century. Not many car companies began as bicycle makers, but before the turn of the 20th century, Ramblers were exactly that—bicycles. By 1902, Thomas Jeffrey and his son Charles sold their bicycle company and decided to sell cars based on one Charles built in 1897. They retained the right to the Rambler name, however, and the first car from the company that later became Nash was a little one-cylinder car called Rambler. In 1902, with about 1,500 copies produced, it was the second highest selling car in the U.S., just behind the curved-dash Oldsmobile.

The first iteration was very conservative, but by 1904 such niceties as a steering wheel (the thought of a steering wheel being an extra-cost option brings a smile to my face) and a two-cylinder engine were standard on all Ramblers. In 1914, the company name was changed to Jeffrey, to honor the departed Thomas Jeffrey who died suddenly in 1910.

Things were going swimmingly for the Jeffrey Company, until Charles himself took a swim. Charles Jeffrey booked passage on a ship called the Lusitania, which got in the way of a German torpedo. Jeffrey survived the sinking of the Lusitania but decided that life was too short to spend making cars. He sold his company to Charles Nash and retired to smell the roses at the ripe old age of forty. From 1918 until 1954, when Nash and

An MIB perfect Nash emblem lighter from 1946. Even the insert has no abrasion scratches. $325-350

A 1952 Golden Anniversary Nash in used condition. The paint is gone, and because the case was steel instead of brass (due to the Korean War) the recessed areas have corrosion in them. It appears to have been re-hinged as well. In mint condition, this is a very valuable lighter. *Courtesy Kenneth Nickolai.* $250-300 mint; $60-75 as is.

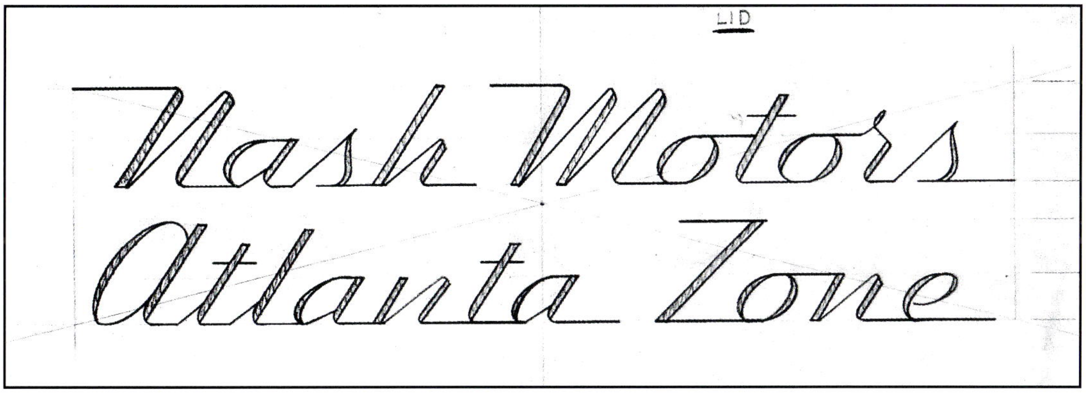

This cardboard was used to make the lid of the previous lighter.

Hudson joined hands to form American Motors, Nash had the most efficient independent company, rarely losing money and always producing high quality products.

Nash innovations included the perfection of the air-conditioning system first used by Packard. Before Nash, air-conditioning systems were located in the trunk, and were big and inefficient. Nash moved the whole shebang under the hood, a method of cooling so advanced it is still used today. The Rambler name was re-born in 1950, and when the Nash name was killed at the end of the 1957 model year, Rambler continued as the name for the entire American Motors line of cars. The Rambler name was laid to rest at the end of the 1969 model year. AMC was the name on American Motors products for the rest of its history.

Zippo artwork advertising Nash is more varied than for any of the other independents, but Rambler lighters all refer to the post-Nash era. Nash Zippo lighters were made extensively in the early 1950s, though "extensively," when referring to any independent, still means "rare."

An undated Nash logo.

A re-painted Nash lighter, based on the previous cardboard. The re-painting looks out of place, because of the corrosion on the case. *Courtesy Parker Collection.* $50-60 as is.

An undated Nash Service logo.

This Nash lighter is a much better candidate for a repaint, because the case is very clean. *Courtesy Richard Weinstein.* $60-75 as is.

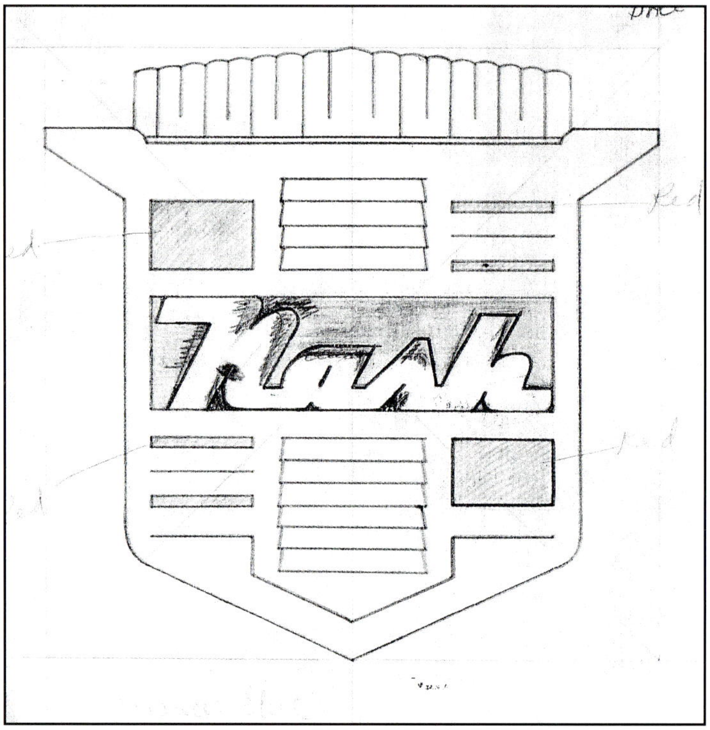

A Nash shield. Note the alterations that have been made to the artwork. The Nash lighter in the "brassing" section is based on this cardboard.

Airflyte Theatre was a radio show sponsored by Nash.

Hudson

The Hudson Motor Car Company was born in 1909 and was named after J.L. Hudson, a Detroit department store owner who provided the initial funding, his name and, apparently, nothing else. Roy Dikeman Chapin and Harry E. Coffin led the company. (One wonders how many "all-new four-door Coffins" would have sold.) The new Hudson Model 20 was a smash. A new car sales record was set in 1910, Hudson's first full year of production.

Over the next forty-five years Hudson developed the reputation for quality, safety, speed and reliability that still makes them coveted cars today. Though the last true Hudson was built in 1954, the Hudson name was put on cars using Nash bodies from 1955-1957. Excellent brakes, a light clutch and true center steering made Hudsons "driver's cars" for their entire history. In 1948, Hudson introduced the finest cars to ever wear the Hudson name. They were called collectively, Step-Downs, because passengers stepped down into the car, instead of up, as in other cars. The Step-Down design was so advanced, all cars today use the same basic system.

By the early 1950s, Hudson sales had begun to fall, and the writing was on the wall: Merger. Hudson merged with Nash, and American Motors dropped the Hudson and Nash names at the end of the 1957 model year.

A mint Hudson Zippo lighter. *Courtesy Ed Pinedo.* $300-350

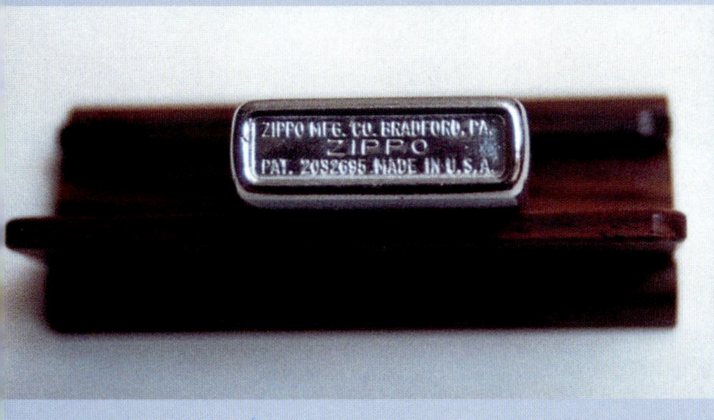

This Hudson lighter has a logo similar to the lighter on the far left, though the remaining paint is red. Nellie Holmes was a New York Hudson dealer. $100-125 as is.

Two interesting MIB Hudson lighters with the same logo. However, one is unpainted and the other one has the usual red. *Courtesy Ken Poynter & Richard Weinstein.* $300-350

The chrome is almost worn through on this lighter. *Courtesy Ken Poynter*. $75-85 as is.

This lighter might never have had paint. Despite its condition, this lighter is valuable to Hudson collectors. *Courtesy Ken Poynter.* $75-85 as is.

A mint text-only Hudson lighter. It is worth less because the artwork is plain. *Courtesy Ken Poynter.* $200-250

An original emblem Hudson lighter. Compare this lighter with the "fake" in the emblem section. *Courtesy Ken Poynter.* $200-250 as is.

Rambler

Two 1961 Rambler lighters: one mint, the other about 85%. Mint: $150-175; 85%: $80-100

This lighter dates from 1963. The rule probably comes from the same year, as they have the same paint scheme. These examples are slightly different from the previous two lighters, which are 1961 examples. Note the difference in the text color. *Rule courtesy Tony Zamisch, lighter Courtesy Parker Collection.*

The entire Rambler line won Motor Trend's Car Of The Year award in 1963.

A very unique logo on a mint 1963 lighter. This logo may have been custom-designed for the individual dealer. *Courtesy Richard Weinstein.* $150-175

A 1963 Rambler slim. The Rambler logo appears in several variations in this section, but each has been verified original. All Rambler items are rare and valuable. $40-50

AMC

In 1996, I visited the International Lighter Museum in Guthrie, Oklahoma, and went through every single lighter in the Museum, looking for AMC Zippo lighters. This was the only one I found. It is unused. $175+

An AMC Javelin lighter. The Javelin was a muscle car, and one of the best all-around cars AMC ever built. *Courtesy Tony Zamisch.* This lighter is not mint, but is still valued at well over $200+.

A 1976 Slim Zippo lighter. The Buyer Protection Plan was the best warranty in the auto industry. *Courtesy Tony Zamisch.* $30-40

Bricklin

Among the modern short-lived makes of American cars, the Bricklin of 1974-75 deserves special mention. Malcolm Bricklin wanted to make the safest sports car in the U.S. The Safety Vehicle 1, or SV-1, was offered in the five most visible colors on the road, and boasted—or suffered from—gull-wing doors, which took eight weary seconds to open or close.

Unfortunately, build quality of the SV-1 was mediocre at best, due in part to the fact that the assembly line work force was drawn from among the unemployed people of the rural Canadian province where Bricklins were built. Essentially farmers, hunters and outdoorsmen, they lacked the training necessary for efficient auto assembly and presented some unique problems for management. For instance, absenteeism was almost total when hunting season opened.

In two years of production, fewer then 2,900 Bricklins were made, including a few re-numbered as 1976 models. Bricklin supposedly included not smoking in his pantheon of safety items, so his cars lacked the ashtray and cigarette lighter found in other cars. It is far more likely that it was cheaper to just omit them. Why else would Zippo have made a run of Bricklin lighters? The story goes that a lighter was given to each Bricklin purchaser, but they seem to be far more rare than that. Both slim and full-size Zippo lighters were made with the Bricklin logo.

An interesting side note is that a fellow named John Z. DeLorean was interested in both the car and the operation and offered to help. Nothing came of the negotiations, and DeLorean eventually built his own stainless steel gull-wing door car, complete with standard ashtray and cigarette lighter, until he allegedly got involved with drug trafficking. More novel than the ploys of Davis and Playboy, but no more successful, DeLorean and his car drove into history in the early 1980s, the last new car company in the United States.

Bricklin lighters are very rare, especially in the full-size version. *Courtesy Richard Weinstein.* $150+

The Bricklin slim lighter, with exactly the same logo. Interestingly, Bricklin Zippo lighters were not made in Canada, though the cars were. Also, this Bricklin slim dates from 1977, though the last cars were actually made in 1975. *Courtesy Parker Collection.* $60-80 as is.

Kaiser-Frazer

A very early Kaiser-Frazer lighter. The Frazer clan complained about the use of the family crest. This three-barrel hinge lighter may date from 1947. None of the original K-F lighters pictured here are mint. $150-175

Another early K-F lighter. Note the difference between the Kaiser emblems. $150-175

Close-ups of two Kaiser emblems. Note basic differences in width and detail. Also note the paint chipping.

A close-up look at two Frazer emblems.

The engraving on this lighter was not done by Zippo Mfg. Look at the condition of the emblems. *Courtesy Mike Muehlberger.* $150-175

This is a 1979 reproduction K-F lighter. Note that it has the earlier Frazer "emblem," but also has the slogan on the back from the later lighter. This example is MIB. $50-60

Many later K-F lighters had this slogan on the back. $150-175

Packard

Packard. Even now, over forty years after the bitter death of the Packard automobile, the name conjures up memories of the most awe-inspiring cars ever built. Packard cars were neither the most expensive (though not far from it), nor the most popular, nor even, perhaps, the best cars on the road during the company's lifetime. But the Packard Motor Car Company created a mystique that has never been equaled by any other car maker. "Made by Gentlemen, Sold by Gentlemen to Gentlemen," if you wished to learn about a Packard, you needed only to "...ask the man who owns one." The power of that slogan is so strong, it has been cleaned up and used in the modern era to flog other, less worthy cars. Somehow, though, "Ask the person who owns one" just doesn't do it for me.

Founded in 1899, by 1900 Packard had the industry's first H-pattern gearshift, and offered a steering wheel. By 1904, Packard was established as a luxury car, with the four-cylinder model K priced at a staggering $7,000.

Throughout the history of Packard, the quality of the cars that bore the proud name was phenomenal. Regardless of the cost, what the buyer drove home in was the most carefully built car available. Even today the door of a Packard car opens and closes with the solid assurance of a bank vault.

Unfortunately, Packard couldn't survive as a luxury marque, making a paltry few thousand cars a year, even as superbly made as they were. The firm's management "harrumphed" at the thought of needing to join forces with another company; but, in 1955 Packard bought Studebaker. The year 1956 was the last for the "true" Packard cars. By the end of the 1958 model year, Packard was gone, after just two seasons of embarrassingly ugly Studebaker-bodied cars using the Packard name.

Early Packard Zippo lighters used simple emblems with the Packard crest, easily identifiable by the cormorant on the top. No Packard metalliques are known. Some Packard lighters are in the Zippo Museum. They are not for sale. I asked. A Packard Zippo lighter is one of the great treasures of automobile Zippo advertising, and any one would be a "keeper."

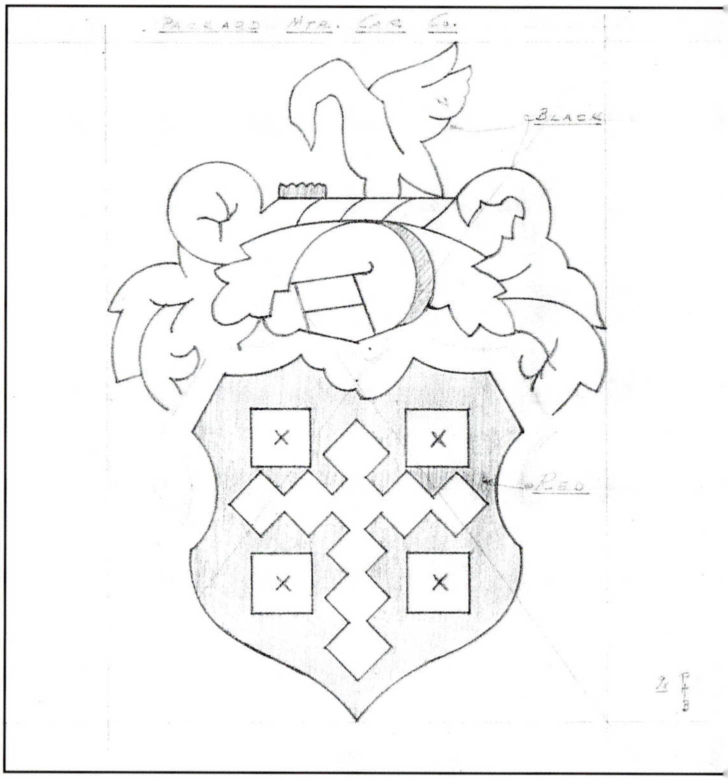

A 1952 cardboard of the Packard crest. The cormorant is an immediate signal that this is a Packard logo.

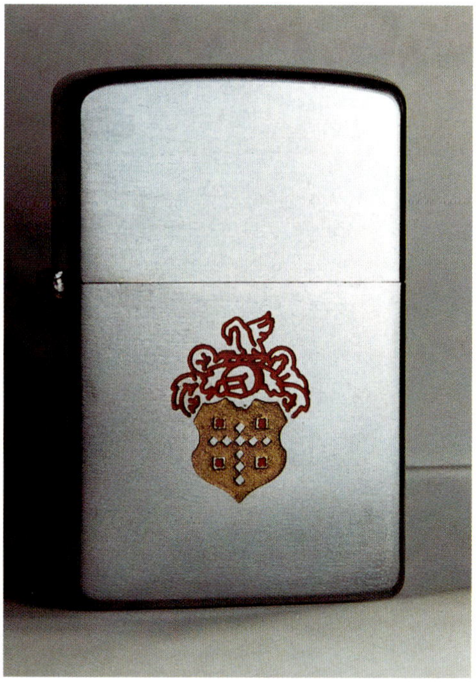

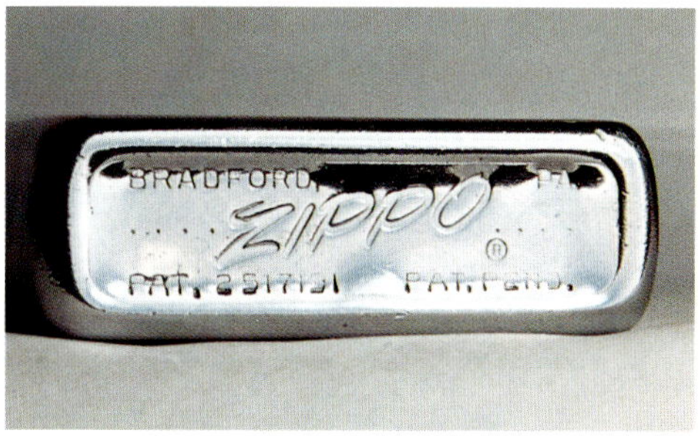

Compare the color indications on the previous cardboard to this owner repainted lighter. The lighter is from 1956, so the color scheme might well have changed. $75-100

A Packard cardboard from 1951. During Packard's entire history, the lettering of the Packard name never changed.

A lovely lighter based on the previous cardboard, with text added. $75-100 as is.

A simple, yet very impressive, Packard ad.

A tired #203 Packard lighter. It has been re-hinged at least five times and has zero paint, but is still a Packard Zippo lighter. What a combination for the lover of quality. $60-75

Studebaker

Studebaker was a builder of "horsed carriages" for many years before delving into the realm of the self-propelled. When the name Studebaker was attached to *horseless* carriages, the first were electrically powered. Early internal combustion engines were desperately inefficient, so electric and steam power plants were a viable alternative. (Stanley Steamer, for instance, lasted into the mid-1920s.)

During Studebaker's lifetime, lower-priced "companion cars" were introduced to increase market share and product mix. Each foray seemed cursed, however.

The low-priced Erskine 6, named for then corporate president Albert Erskine, was introduced in 1927, with a low price of $945. At the same time, Ford announced its new Model A ... for $525.

In mid-1930, Erskines were imaginatively renamed "the Studebaker 6." The Depression almost claimed Studebaker (as personal bankruptcy would doom the Erskine's namesake, who killed himself in 1933). Studebaker tried again in 1932. The new car

A 1953 Studebaker dealership cardboard.

was called the Rockne, named after Knute Rockne, the great football coach. Rockne was promptly killed in a plane crash. The name was discontinued at the end of 1933, not because of any perceived jinx, but because of the ubiquitous Model A, which cost $150 dollars less than the Rockne.

After W.W.II, Studebaker, like all car companies, sold every car it made; but, hindsight shows the first signs of the problem that eventually killed all the independents: price. Studebakers were more expensive than the low-priced cars from the "big three." The post-war buyer's market faded by 1950, and some poor (a tactfully chosen word) management decisions led to the downward spiral of the nation' s oldest car company. After Packard bought Studebaker, and the Packard name was discontinued, the firm fled to Canada to die an agonizingly slow death by 1966.

Studebaker advertised for many years on Zippo lighters, with its logo appearing either as etch/paint or as an attached emblem. The Zippo Museum has several Studebaker emblems on display, symbols of one of the last of the independent car makers.

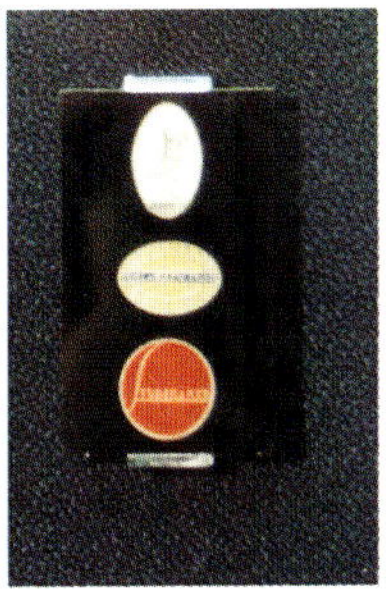

A Studebaker metallique in the Zippo Museum.

The logo on these mint lighters is impressive yet simple. *Courtesy Richard Weinstein.* $200-300

Tucker

The history of the auto industry is filled with stories of amazing men, of rags to riches (and of riches to rags), of missed chances and great strokes of luck. The controversial saga of Preston Tucker's car has all of these attributes. Tucker wanted to build a car that was safe, reliable, fast and stylish. He did. That only fifty-one cars were made is blamed on everything from Tucker himself to the U.S. Government to the "big three," who—allegedly—saw him as a serious threat.

Although he was involved in many different pursuits during his career, Tucker's first love was cars. He told his designer, Alex Tremulis, "We have a boss that's bigger than us, and that's the automobile." During W.W.II, while the Air Force was using a rotating gun turret he had designed, Tucker was making plans to produce the most advanced production car ever seen. By 1950, however, Tucker had been acquitted in a highly publicized fraud trial and the car itself was dead.

Never one to give up, Tucker was making arrangements for Brazilian production of the Carioca, a two-seat sports car with free-standing fenders, when he himself died.

Those who doubt Tucker's desire to build a car need only look at some of the features his car had that ended up on later cars: pop-out windshields, doors extending into the roof (eliminating the need for rain gutters), torsion-bar suspension, disc brakes, air-cooling, 24-volt electrical system, and a pivoting headlight, among other things. Some of the innovations of the Tucker, like 24-volt electrics and disc brakes, were natural evolution and would have come anyway; but the fact is, he had them before anyone else in 1948.

Other Tucker ideas were modified for modern use. For instance, most GM cars now have side headlights that come on only during turns, directly traceable to the Tucker. Interestingly, the free-standing fenders to be used on the Carioca also showed up on a production car; take a look at the Plymouth Prowler. A final proof that Tucker did indeed intend to build his car (his accusers claimed his corporation was another "stock scam," not a legitimate car company) is simply this: Anyone who wishes to purchase one of the forty-six or so remaining Tuckers will need over a quarter-million dollars to do so. The most recent Tucker transaction, involving Tucker #45, saw over $346,000 change hands.

A two-page ad for the Tucker. Despite emphasizing safety, Tucker didn't want seat belts in his car.

Following pages: Two interesting print ads from Adcraft. Adcraft sold Zippo lighters with specialty advertising on them, and they ordered the Tucker lighters. The question now rises of whether the Tucker emblem was attached by Zippo MFG or by Adcraft. *Courtesy Mark Boone & Raymond Parmenter.*

Exact Replica

of the Tucker Emblem in Authentic Colors

"**Excitingly handsome**"—that's what you'll say when you see this authentic reproduction of the Tucker Emblem. It's a real piece of jewelry that will be worn with pride by every Tucker representative. Of course, you'll want every one of your organization to have one in his coat lapel at all times. It's a "natural" for starting "Tucker Talk." BE SURE TO WEAR ONE YOURSELF!

This exact replica of the Tucker Emblem is expertly executed in a Gold Plated emblem with true Tucker Colors (red, white, black, and gold). Finished with screw-post and button back. Securely fastens in lapel. Not to be confused with cheap substitutes. Attractively priced.

NO. TC-11

One Lapel Emblem . . **$1.15**	6 Dozen Lots @ **$1.05 each**
Dozen Lots @ **$1.10 each**	12 Dozen Lots @ **$1.00 each**

Prices are Postpaid and include 20% Federal Excise Tax

Send all orders direct, and make checks payable to:

ADCRAFT SALES PROMOTION CO., 9815 GRAND RIVER AVE., DETROIT 4, MICH.

Prices subject to change without notice.

Form No. AS-149 Litho in U.S.A. 5-48

TC-12

THE FAMOUS ZIPPO LIGHTER *Personalized* FOR TUCKER DEALERS

Beautifully finished with the Tucker Emblem in Authentic Colors

May be Engraved With Signatures

You'll take particular pride in using this famous Zippo Lighter with the distinctive Tucker Emblem. Whenever you use or show the lighter it reflects a note of elegance that will win admiration.

These lighters are built to last for years and have the Zippo patented wind-proof shield.

The Tucker Emblem is beautifully engraved, exact in all details — gold plated with fired-enameled colors — it is striking in appearance against the brush-finished lighter.

May be ordered in four different ways—see listing at right.

PRICE LIST

With Emblem Only	TC-12	1 or more	**$2.50** each
With Emblem and 2 or 3 Initials	TC-13	1 or more	**$3.10** each
With Emblem and your own and other signatures	TC-14	1 or more	**$3.10** each
With Emblem and your name and address (3 line limit)	TC-15	50-199	**$2.75** each
		200-399	**2.65** each
		400 & over	**2.50** each

TC-13 REAR VIEW

TC-14 REAR VIEW

TC-15 REAR VIEW

All prices include Federal Excise Tax, f.o.b. Bradford, Pa. and are subject to change without notice.

Send all orders direct, and make checks payable to:

ADCRAFT SALES PROMOTION COMPANY

9815 GRAND RIVER AVENUE, DETROIT 4, MICHIGAN

Form No. AS-150 Litho in U.S.A. 5-48

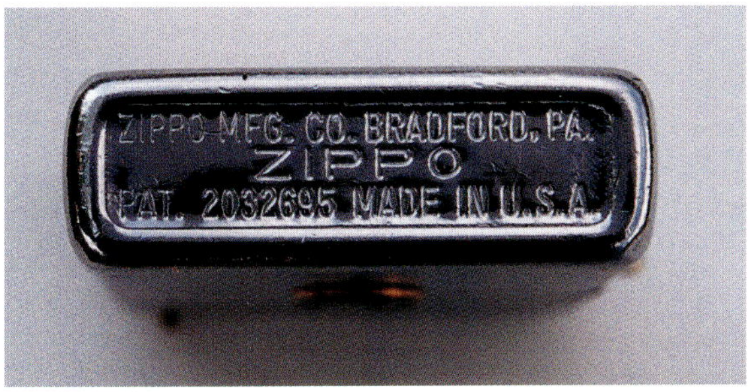

This lighter was a personal gift from Preston Tucker to his secretary, Doris "Dedee" Jordan. Because the back has Zippo engraving, the emblem was probably attached at Zippo. Regardless, the connection to Preston Tucker and the amazing condition make this one of the single most valuable auto lighters ever made. *Courtesy Raymond Parmenter.* No price by request.

Preston Tucker gave this lighter to Dedee Jordan's husband, Al Jordan. The artwork is different, but the engraving of the name is in the same style. Al's lighter came from the west coast, and Dedee's came from the east coast, so these two lighters are re-united in this book after many years. A poignant thought. *Courtesy George Boucher.* No price by request.

A close-up of Al Jordan's signature. Compare the engraving with his wife's lighter. The Tucker car ashtray by itself is extremely valuable. *Courtesy George Boucher*. Ashtray: $1200+. The ashtray was originally offered to dealers for $12.00.

From artwork to lighter.

The first reproduction Tucker lighter. Compare this lighter to Al Jordan's. If mint: $50-75

A "restricted" piece of artwork that was not used.

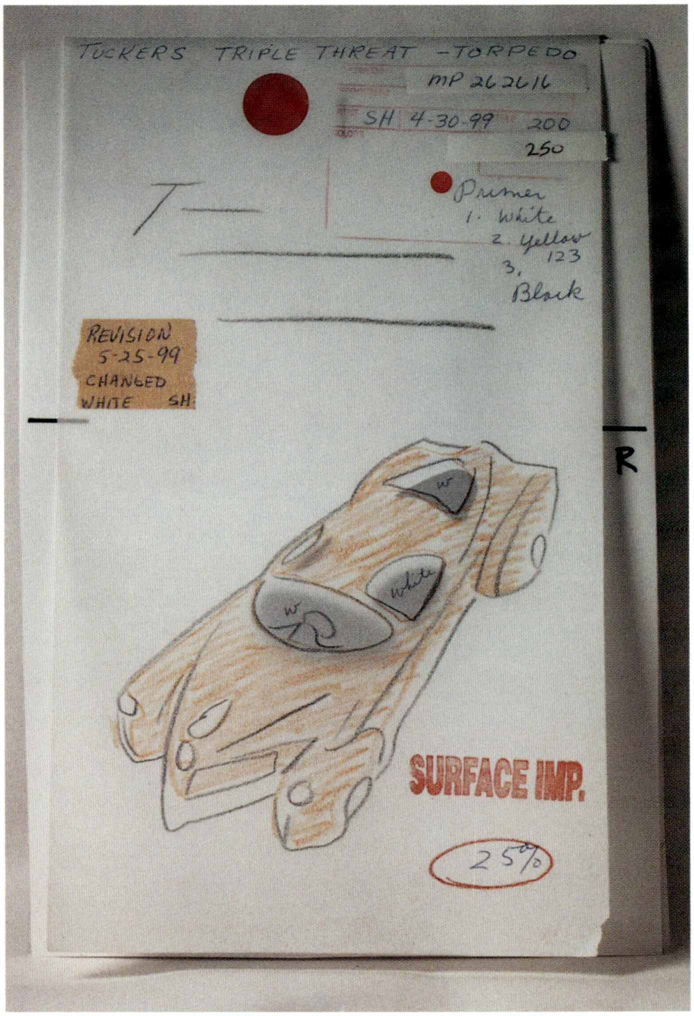

Tucker's original plans were for a center mounted steering wheel.

TORPEDO ON WHEELS

LONG, LOW, and streamlined, the Tucker Torpedo has doors that extend into the top for easier getting in and out. Brakes are of an automatically adjusting type developed originally for racing cars. A new engine can oe installed in 15 minutes when necessary

Engine in rear, all-hydraulic drive make the Tucker a real car of the future

MORE like a Buck Rogers Special than the automobiles we know today, the Tucker Torpedo is scheduled to hit the road sometime in '47. If all goes according to plan, this startling car will incorporate a series of spectacular engineering innovations that conservative auto manufacturers have classified as "at least five or six years off."

Here are some of the highlights of this 126-inch wheelbase vehicle in its present design:

Hydraulic torque converters provide a direct power-transmitting system that does away with the customary clutch, transmission, drive shaft, differential, and rear axle. That eliminates about 800 working parts and saves

OPERATION of car's hydraulic drive is shown in diagram above. Fluid in reservoir (A) flows to pump (B) driven by car's engine. Pump forces fluid through flexible pipes to hydraulic motors (C), which drive rear wheels. Fluid then returns to reservoir for re-use.

62 SCIENCE ILLUSTRATED

The artwork on the tins was done as carefully as on the lighters themselves. *Courtesy Mark Boone.*

A cover story on the Carioca, in the planning stages when Tucker died. Plymouth Prowler, anyone? *Courtesy Mark Boone.*

The Carioca lighter & tin. These reproductions can sell for up to $75.

Trucks

While Ford, Durant, and the gang were busily putting the people of America on wheels, there were other people just as busily trying to put American freight on the road. These companies are the ones who left passenger car making entirely, concentrating on what are now known as "the big rigs." Some companies began as car makers, then moved to the greener and wide-open spaces of the large truck industry simply because the market was expanding. Other companies never made anything else.

Mack Trucks, for instance, was founded in 1900, making it one of the oldest companies in the industry. All Mack made was trucks, big and burly. Some beautiful light-duty trucks were made for a time, but they were too expensive to compete with Ford.

I remember using the phrase, "Built like a Mack truck" before I was even sure what a Mack truck was. The Mack bulldog is one of the most famous logos in the vehicle industry, and has appeared (almost always as an emblem) on many Zippo lighters throughout the years. It is the most common automotive logo I have seen on a Zippo lighter.

Jeffrey also made trucks for the Allies during W.W.I, and almost became a truck maker; however, after Charles Nash bought and re-named the company after himself, Nash made only a small number of light duty trucks for the rest of its life. Studebaker made large trucks as well, especially during W.W.II, but was of course mainly a builder of passenger cars.

After leaving the car business in 1936, Reo made trucks until 1957, when it was acquired by White, along with Autocar and Diamond T. All of these companies appeared on Zippo lighters, as do GMC Truck and Coach, Freightliner, Peterbilt and Kenworth.

White Motor Company started making steam-powered cars in 1901, but after ten years switched to gasoline engines. During W.W.I, White sold 18,000 trucks to the allied countries and decided trucks were good things to build. Eventually, White became the largest truck maker in the U.S.

A Mack truck lighter from the late 1930s, on display in the Zippo Museum. $400-600

A very rare engraved Mack lighter. *Courtesy Michael Gover.* $125-150

A 1962 Mack slim. The emblem has been polished. *Courtesy Parker Collection.* $20-30

A 1965 lighter, with the same round emblem, unpolished. *Courtesy Parker Collection.*

A 1973 cardboard of the Mack bulldog.

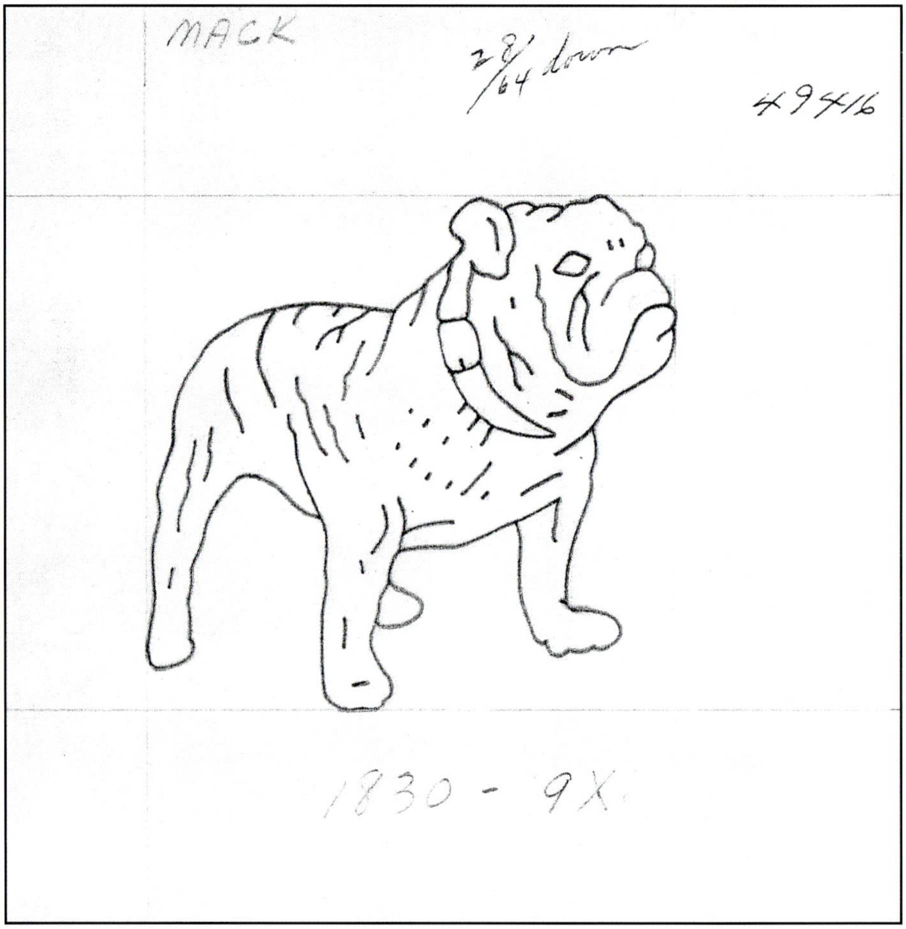

Another 1965 lighter, but with a different emblem. *Courtesy Parker Collection.*

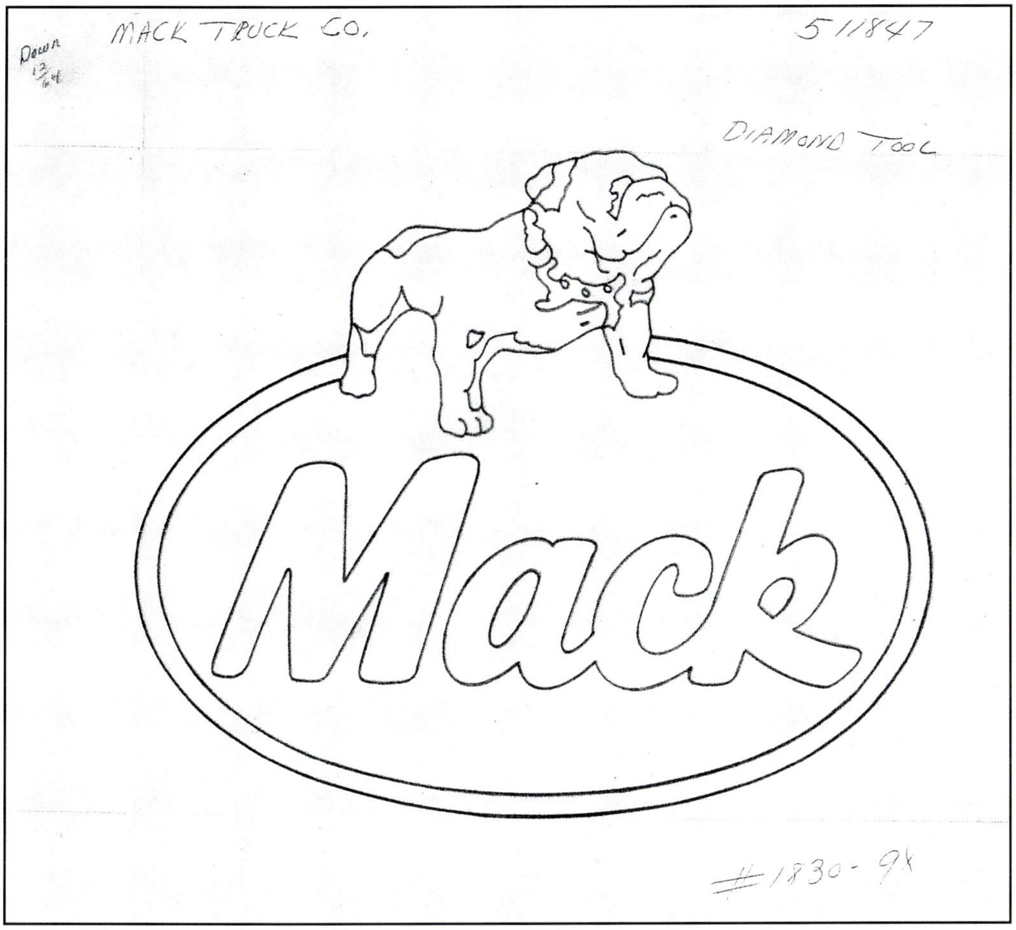

An undated cardboard. "Diamond tool" was a process of engraving the brass before the lighter was plated. The recesses were unpainted, much like in the modern "luster etch" finish. It was often used on sterling silver lighters.

The artwork on this slim was probably custom-ordered by this particular dealer. It has about 75% paint. *Courtesy Rickie Lee Spence.* $20-30

An emblem on a 1974 lighter. Mack used many different emblems. $30-40

Two new lighters. Each is mint. $25-30

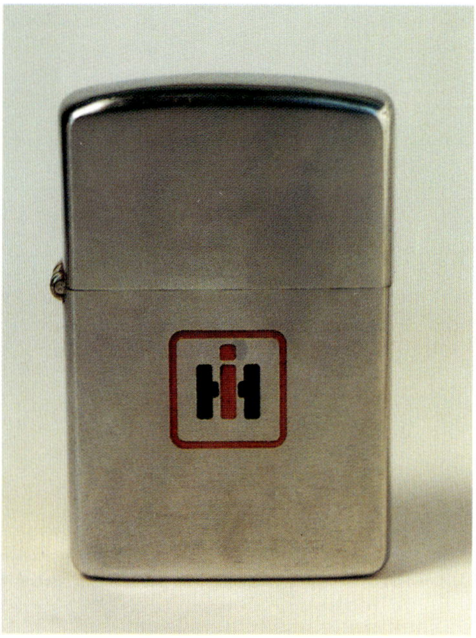

A mint IH lighter. The case is mint, anyway. The insert was switched for a correct used one before I bought it. *Always check the insert.* $100-125

A re-hinged 1966 IH lighter. The large emblem is on the reverse, and the owner's initials are engraved (not by Zippo) on the obverse. It is uncommon to find the emblem on the back. $40-50

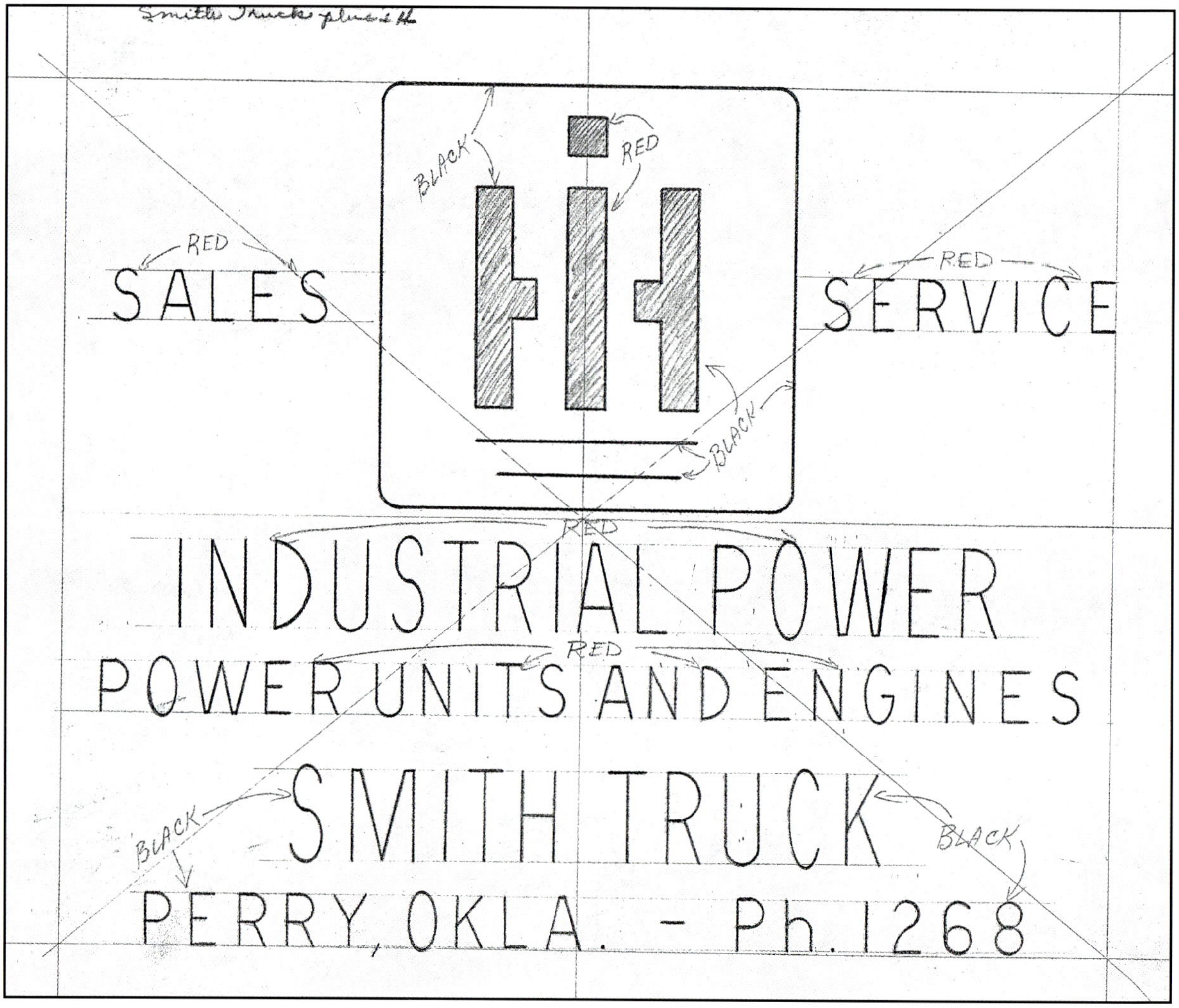

A cardboard for an International Harvester dealer in Oklahoma. Note the four-digit phone number.

This #203 IH lighter has seen an awful lot of harvesting. Note the hinge is missing a barrel. There is some paint left in the logo. *Courtesy Parker Collection.* $15-20

A MIB, highly detailed IH tractor lighter from 1959. The insert is a correct centered 2517191 insert. A terrific lighter. $90-100

Two 1973 Kenworth cardboards. Each cardboard refers to the "diamond tool" process. Note the written reminder for "no color."

A 1957 Diamond T lighter. *Courtesy Parker Collection.* $100-125

A 1966 Diamond T lighter. Compare this example with the 1957 lighter. $50-75

This MIB Freightliner was produced in Canada. Because the bottom surface of a slim is so small, they have no special Canadian stamp. The insert, however, does have a stamp unique to Canadian lighters. Also, the box and paperwork have French and English text. $45-55

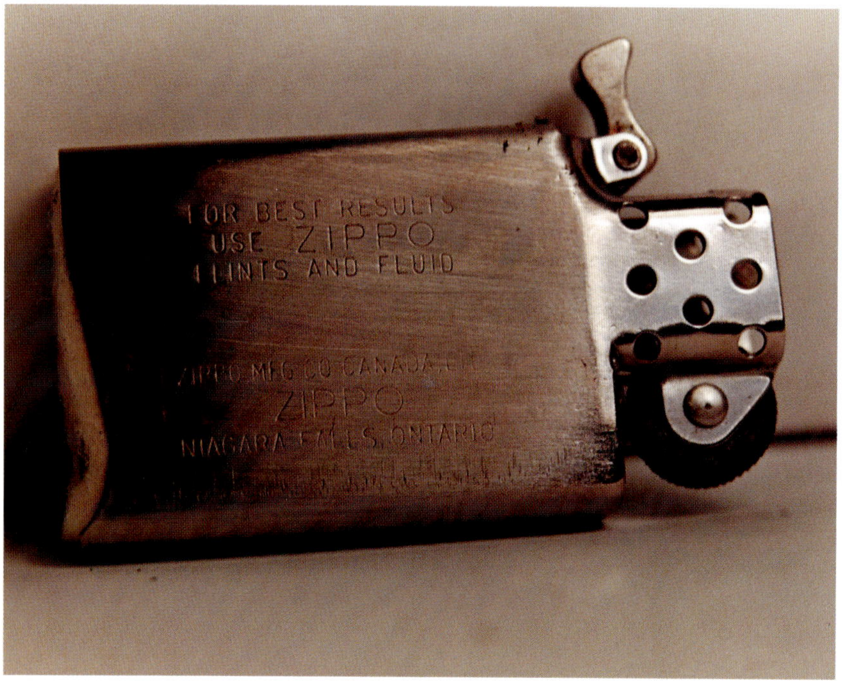

A 1962 Reo slim. The engraving doesn't appear to be by Zippo. *Courtesy Parker Collection.* $30-40

This #203 Reo has about 95% paint. *Courtesy Parker Collection.* $75-100

A highly detailed Reo lighter with 90-95% paint. The engraving on the back is by Zippo. Despite the paint loss, this is a beautiful lighter. *Courtesy Parker Collection.* $125-150

Two Reo emblem lighters. Both are #203 lighters, but only one (the ligher viewed straight on) is a three-barrel. $50-75

Two #203 lighters based on the previous cardboard. Neither has any dealership information. By the time these lighters were made, White was the nation's largest truck maker. Note the difference in the thickness of the black in the circle and the text. *Courtesy Parker Collection.*

A pre-1940 White Superpower lighter in the Zippo Museum. $400-600

An undated White cardboard. Dealers could add dealership information or order lighters with the logo alone.

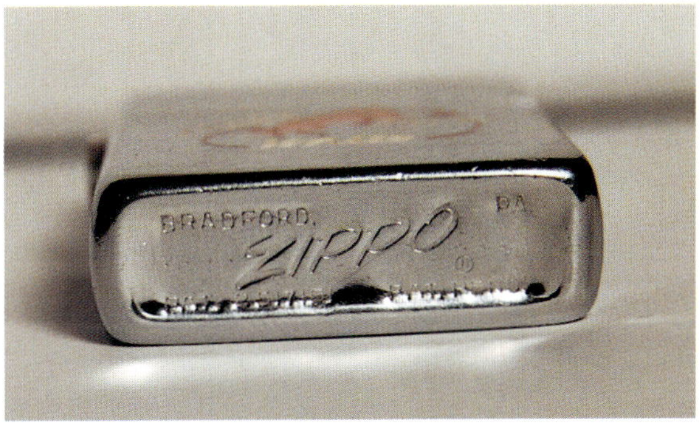

A 1955 lighter. Note the date code. *Courtesy Parker Collection.* $75-100

By 1958, White had purchased almost all the major truck companies, including Autocar, acquired in 1953. This logo was also ordered on sterling silver slim lighters. *Courtesy Parker Collection.* $75-100

This well used 1956-57 slim has the same logo as the previous lighter, with about 35% paint. *Courtesy Parker Collection.* $15-20 as is.

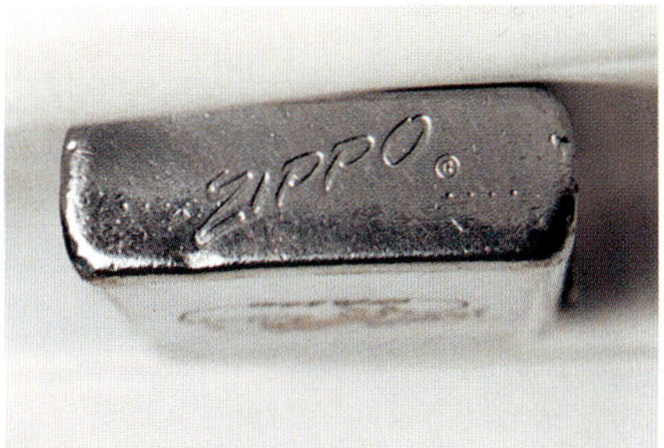

Above: A beautiful 1959 White Autocar slim. $40-50

Right: This cardboard was probably redrawn because the vehicles needed updating. It clearly shows the White pioneered "cab-over-engine" design.

Imports

In 1948, a boat sailed across the sea and dropped off two Volkswagens. Then the boat sailed back to Germany. A few Austins from England, various low-production sports cars, and some ultra-expensive luxury cars from Rolls Royce and Mercedes also made it across the Great Water, but the total was hardly enough to even be noticed by the American car makers. Clearly, Americans were buying American. Not, perhaps, from patriotic pride or a sense of isolationism, but because American cars were big, fast, comfortable, thirsty: just what Americans wanted. A post-war magazine ad for the English Austin pleaded, "Let's take the Austin!" and Americans replied, "let's not."

Everyone had money, and who wanted a little four-seat econobox in 1948? Not Americans, not then anyway, though times have changed a bit since those halcyon days, and a few more Volkswagens were sold over the ensuing years.

Modern Zippo lighters emblazoned with Citroen, Honda or Toyota are fairly common, and there is a series of Mercedes-Benz lighters in the Zippo line. Older Zippo lighters with foreign car companies are rare and desirable, with the humble VW perhaps topping the list.

Many car Zippo lighters are made for sale in the company's home country, but for various reasons are not available in the U.S. In recent years, Zippo has sponsored racing cars in both Japan and Korea. A line of Zippo products focuses on these cars, but all of them are for sale only in their respective markets, and are rare in the U.S.

An Audi slim, owned by the Zippo Museum. $40-50

A brand-new BMW lighter. *Courtesy Ed Pinedo.* $30-35

This car looks like a Pontiac or Olds from 1953-54. *Courtesy Zippo Mfg.* $40-50

A lovely Citroen lighter, with the preparatory artwork. Notice the changes made in the lid, from red screen to luster etch. It is not clear if this is a reproduction of an original Citroen lighter. $40-50

Citroen taxi art.

A Citroen lighter's preparatory artwork. Artwork was often revised according to the buyer's wishes.

A Fiat lighter from 1983.
Courtesy Zippo Mfg. $40-50

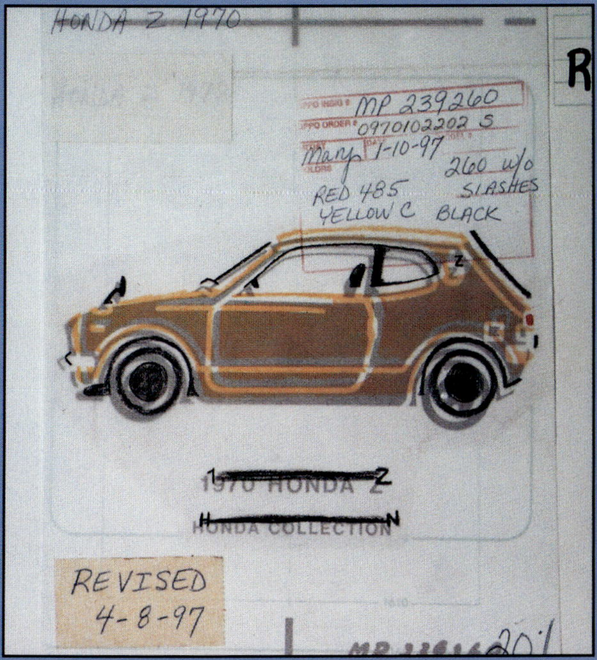

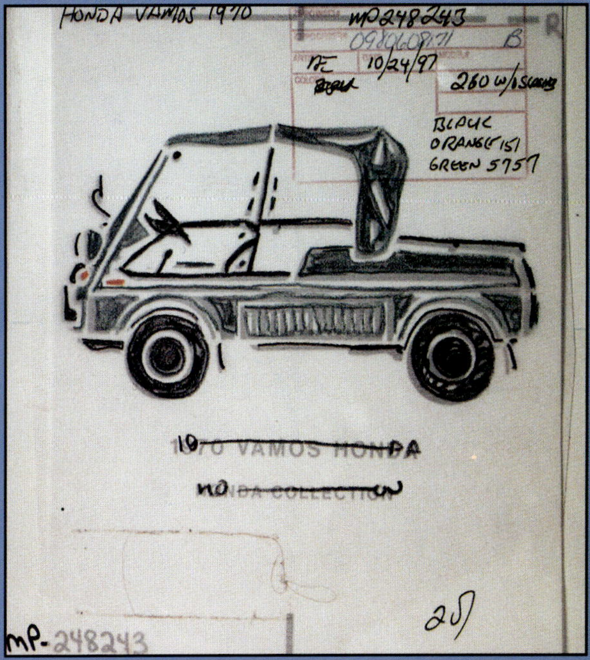

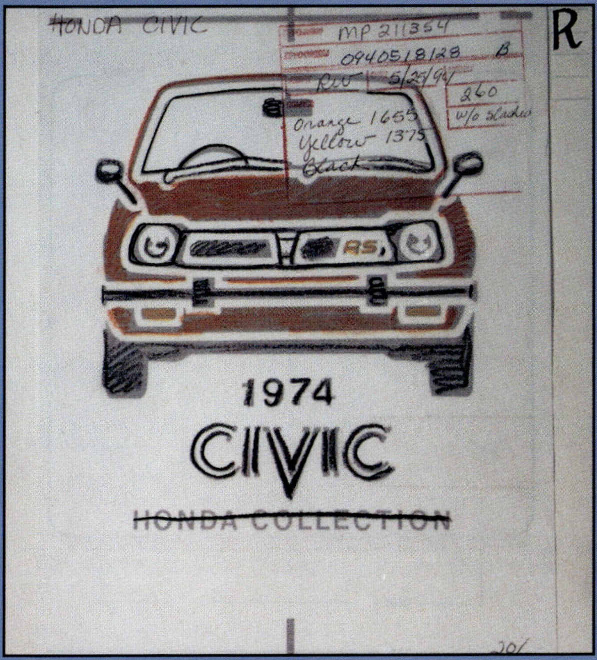

A Honda artwork series. Only the Civic was imported to the U.S. These are probably meant for sale in Japan only.

Two detailed Fiat cars.

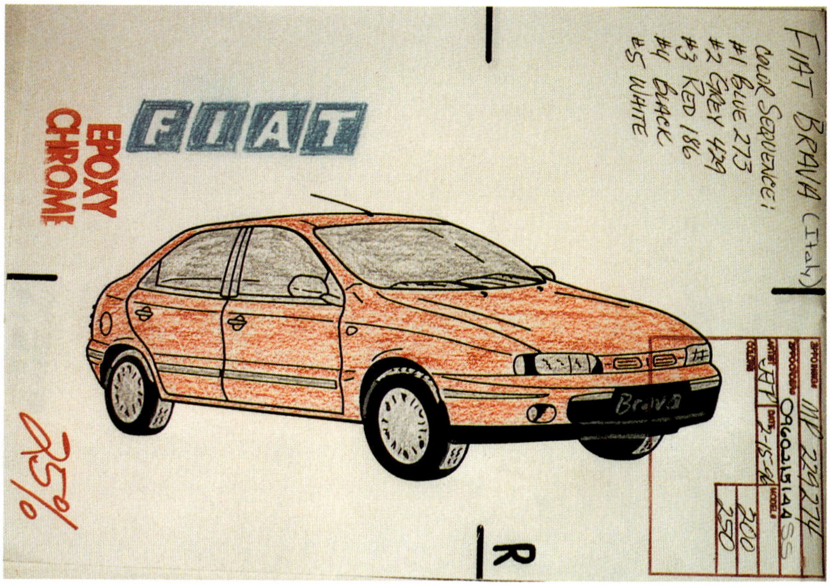

Two cardboards from the same dealer. The Jaguar logo is the same in both pictures. The nameplates are separate cardboards that were taped in place. Apparently, this dealership changed or added owners. Note the "diamond tool" finish.

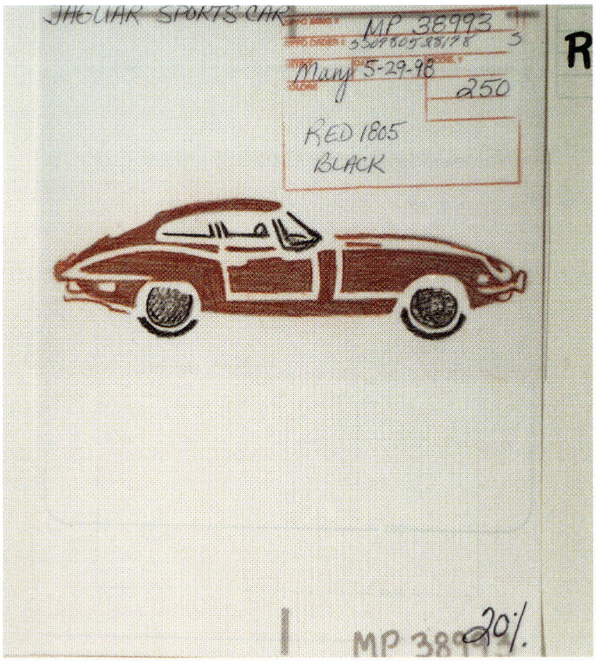

Jaguar artwork.

A 1971 Lotus. It has seen a lot of use, but still looks pretty good. $30-35

A brass MG lighter. Compare the various emblems in this section. $35-40

Artwork showing the new SLK, a retractable hardtop convertible.

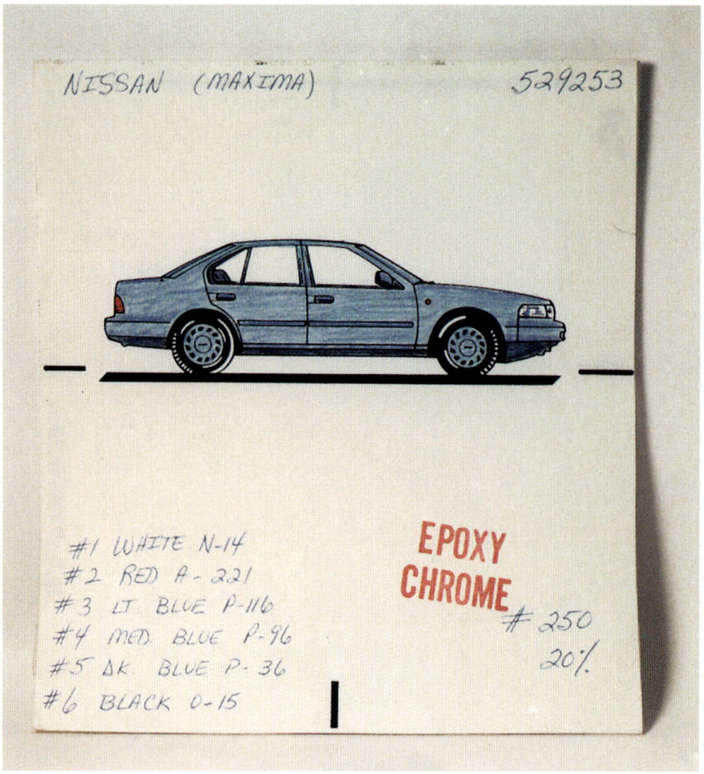

Nissan artwork.

A very detailed 1968 Saab lighter. This is a valuable piece because it depicts an actual Saab. $125-150

Two Porsche lighters. Note the difference between the color schemes. The color version is more valuable. $35-45

Three Toyota Lighters. $40

A Solido VW Zippo van. Sold in Germany, rare in the U.S. $75-100

The VW logo on two cardboards, one from 1955.

The VW logo on this 1970 lighter was blue, and the dealer name was probably black. This lighter has an incorrect insert. $25-30 as is.

A 1963 lighter, probably blue with a black surround. *Courtesy Parker Collection.* $50-60 as is.

A MIB VW slim with an odd emblem, in the Zippo Museum. $40

A mint 1958 VW lighter with an incorrect insert. This logo, which includes a Beetle, is rare. $150-175 with correct insert.

Recent VW artwork.

Modern black and white VW artwork.

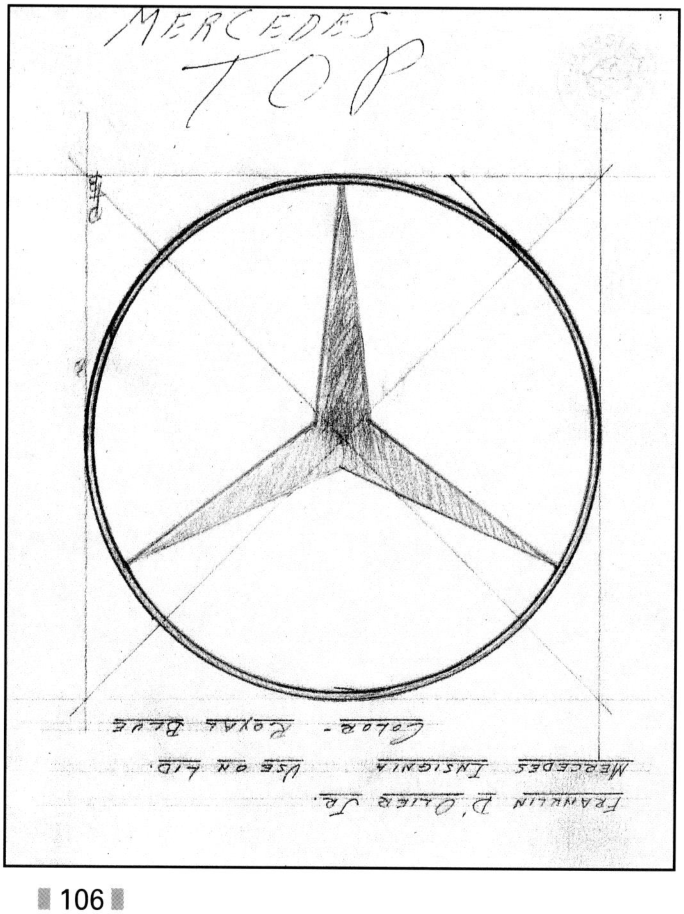

A Mercedes cardboard from 1953.
It also calls for engraving on the lid.

Zippo sponsored racing cars.

NIFTY SERVE
RÄZO
Zippo
23
Avalon
TRAMPIO

T.Hara
Zippo
RÄZO
produced by CAR MATE
11
ATLUS
TRAMPIO
BP

TRAMPIO
11
BP
Zippo
HONDA

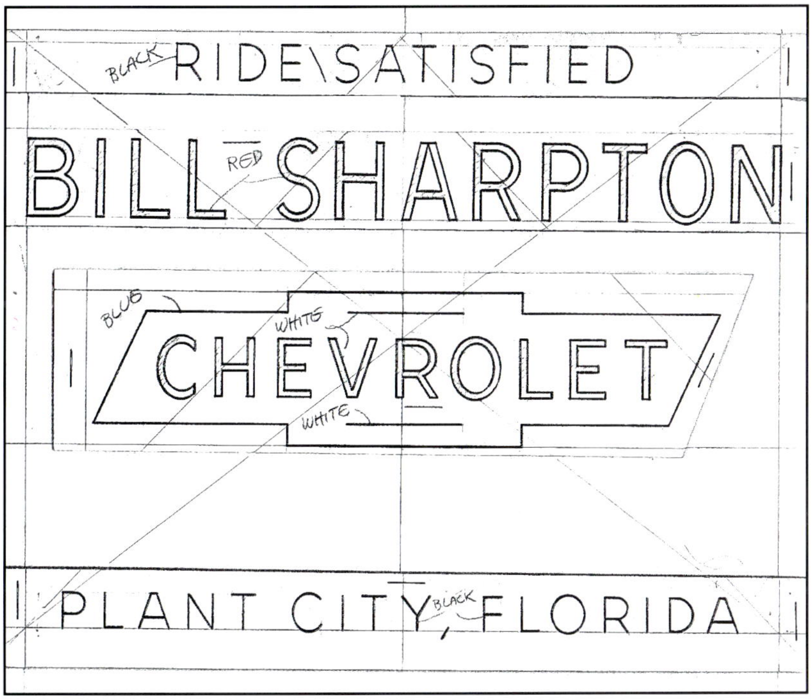

This cardboard is layered. The basic Chevrolet logo is in the center and the dealer information has been added. This basic Chevrolet cardboard was used on many Chevrolet lighters.

Chevrolet

A well-worn basic logo Chevrolet. This lighter probably dates from 1947. *Courtesy Mike Meuhlberger.* $30-40

A typical MIB Chevrolet lighter with address. *Courtesy Ed Pinedo.* $200-250

HANSON
CHEVROLET
COMPANY
DETROIT

CHEVROLET
MT. VERNON
MOTOR CO.
PHONE NO. 1
MT. VERNON, OHIO

PALMER
CHEVROLET
CONNELLSVILLE, PA.

CHEVROLET
BROOKLYN
CHEVROLET
SH 5610

HAL HALSTEAD
CHEVROLET
EDGEWATER
CHEVROLET, INC.
5417 DETROIT AVE.

CHEVROLET
KLINE
CHEVROLET
SALES CORP.

CHEVROLET
GILBERT BROS.
MONTOURSVILLE
&
MUNCY, PA.

CHEVROLET
GRIFFIN AUTO CO.

CHEVROLET
EWING
CHEVROLET, INC.
CANTON, OHIO

Left: All are #203 lighters. Note that, although there is some color variation, the basic logo is the same: outline only. *Courtesy Mike Meuhlberger, Michael Gover, Ed Pinedo, Parker Collection.* $200-225, if MIB

A 1953-55 lighter. Again, the logo is the same, with the slash lines above & below the Chevrolet name. *Courtesy Parker Collection.* $150-175

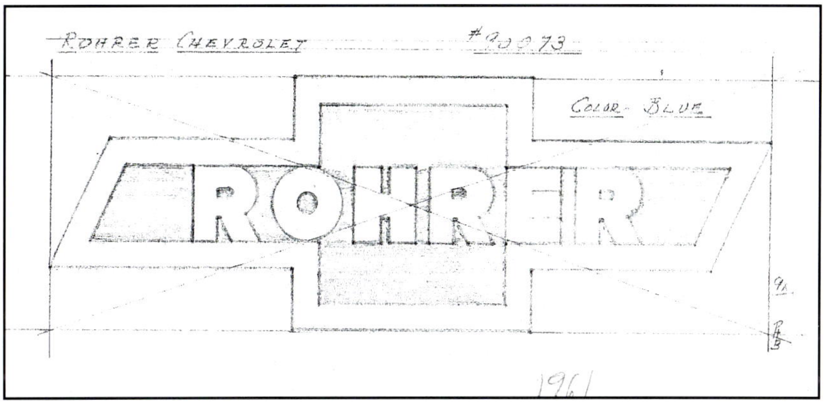

Two cardboards, one of them from 1961, the other undated, but with the same stamp as on the previous lighters. Note the logo color differences.

These lighters were made between 1960-66. Note the difference in the logo. *Courtesy Parker Collection.*

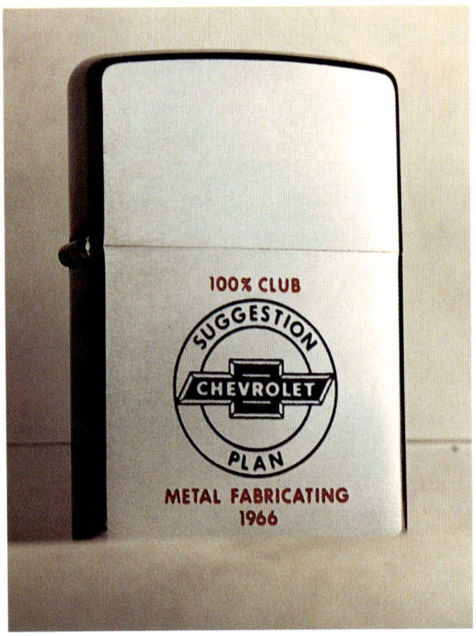

From 1968. *Courtesy Parker Collection.*

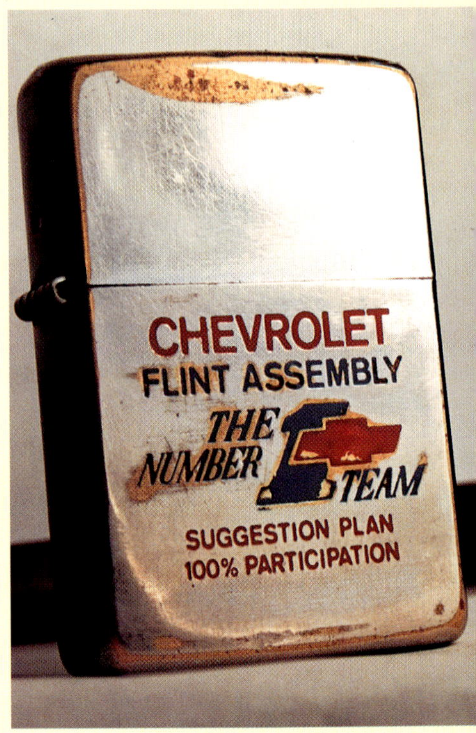

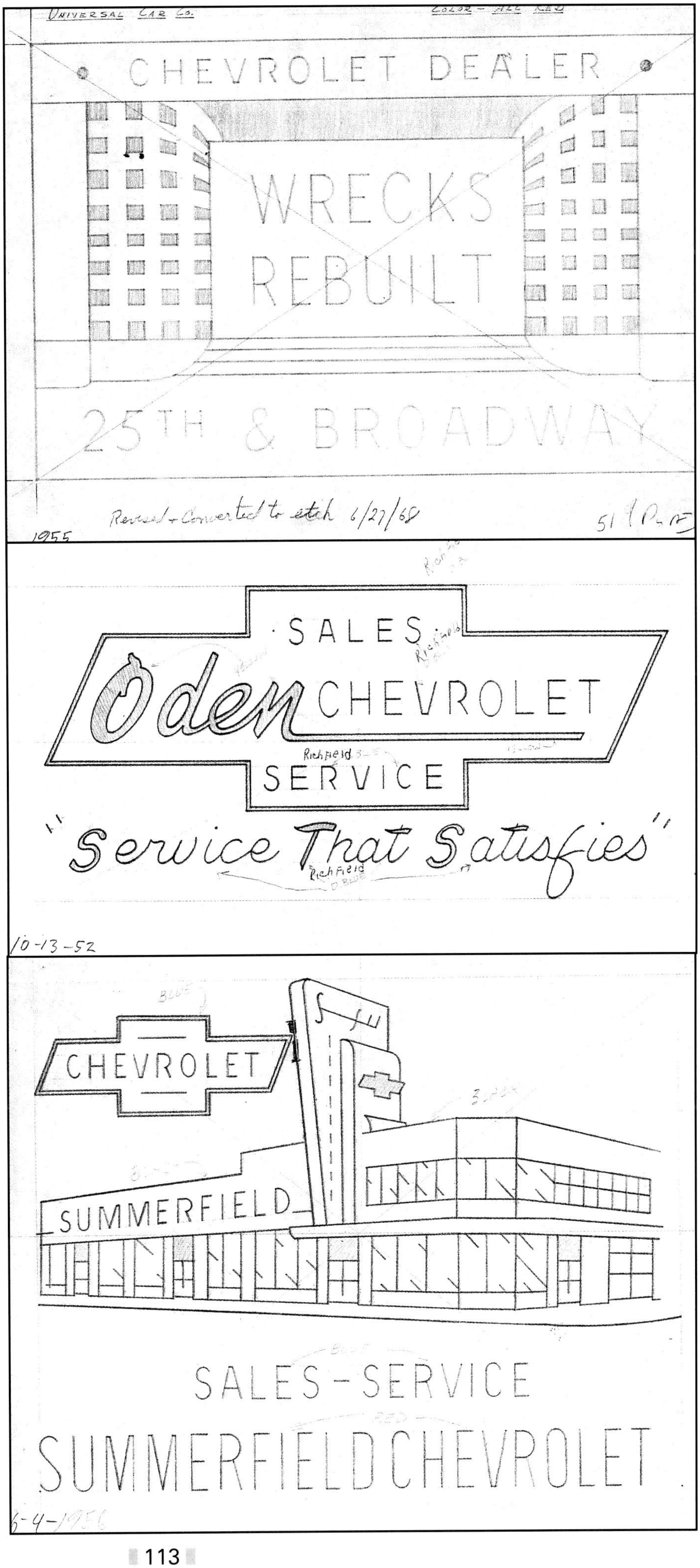

Three dealership cardboards. The detail is impressive, even though none has more than three colors. Complex art is less dependent on multiple colors for interest.

A 1962 Stinn lighter and a 1976 White lighter. Compare the White logo with the Jaguar cardboard. Despite having only two colors, each of the lighters is interesting. *Courtesy Parker Collection.* $125-150, $75-100 respectively.

Two 1968 Corvette slim lighters. The paint scheme includes both gloss and matte black. Car lighters advertising the cars themselves are extremely rare, with fewer than 10 in this entire book. Each of these lighters is desirable, despite the wear. *The better condition lighter is Courtesy Parker Collection.* $40-50, $20-30

A 1959 full-size, and a 1981 slim. *Courtesy Parker Collection.* NP

A complete set of Corvette series lighters. This is the only correct display panel for these lighters, and is worth $35-45 by itself, if mint. The series with panel is rare, because most lighters were sold singly, after which the panel was discarded. $250-275, for the full set.

Corvettes through the years. Note the midnight chrome, new for 1992. *Courtesy Zippo Mfg.* $30-40

Corvette® 1953 - 1993

Corvette®-1957

Corvette®-1963

Corvette®-1969

Corvette®-1978

Some of the artwork for the Corvette series.
Note the many alterations.

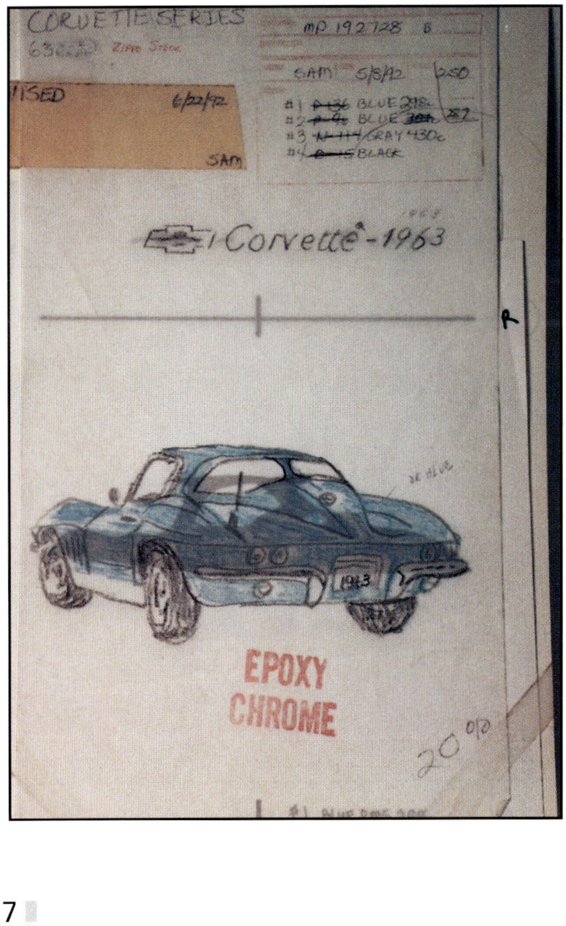

CORVETTE SERIES 1968
Zippo Stock
MP192730 B
5-8-92
250
#1 GRAY
#2 Yellow PMS 122
#3 BLACK PMS
Corvette - 1969
R
EPOXY
CHROME
Revised
6-30-92
Revised
6-19-92

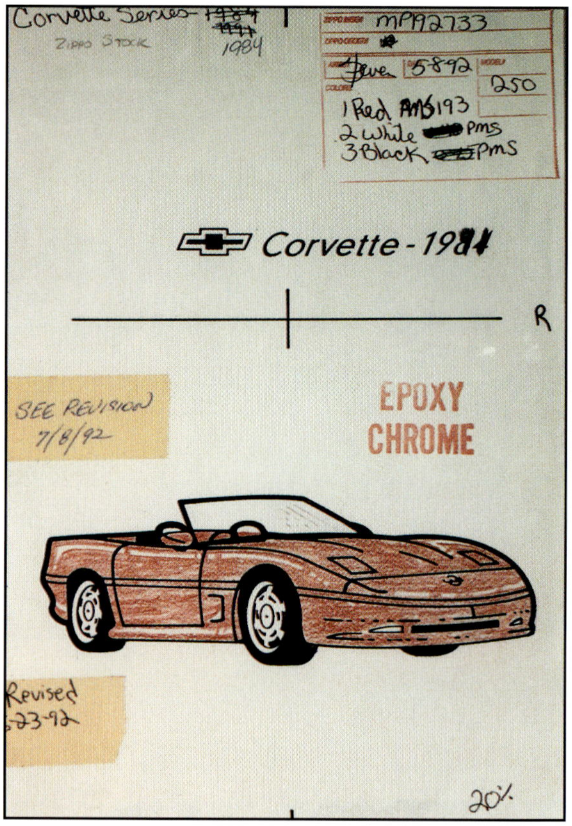
Corvette Series 1984
Zippo Stock
MP192733
5-8-92
250
1 Red PMS 193
2 White PMS
3 Black PMS
R
SEE REVISION
7/8/92
EPOXY
CHROME
Revised
20%

Corvette Series 1986
Zippo Stock
MP 192733 B
Revised
7-8-92
JB
JB
7-8-92
250
1. PMS 431 Gray
2. PMS 193 Red
3. PMS Black
R
REVISION
(YEAR FROM 1984-86)
EPOXY
CHROME
20%

Corvette Series 1991
Zippo Stock
JB
5-8-92
250
1. PMS 425 Gray
2. PMS 193 Red
3. PMS White
4. PMS Black
Corvette - 1991
R
EPOXY
CHROME
REV'D
6-19-92
20%

Two different logos for the 1957 'Vette.

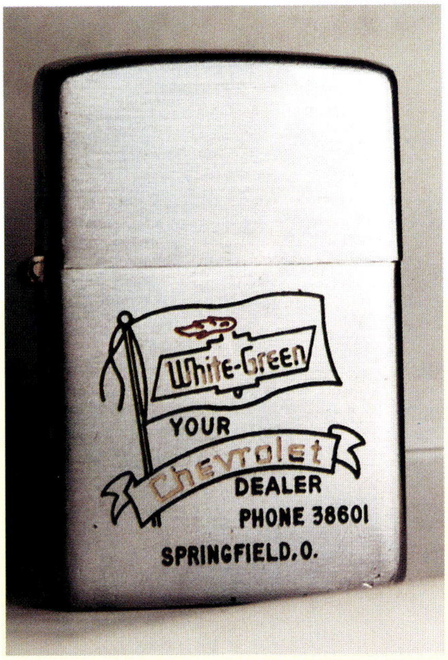

#203 dealership logo lighters.
$125-150

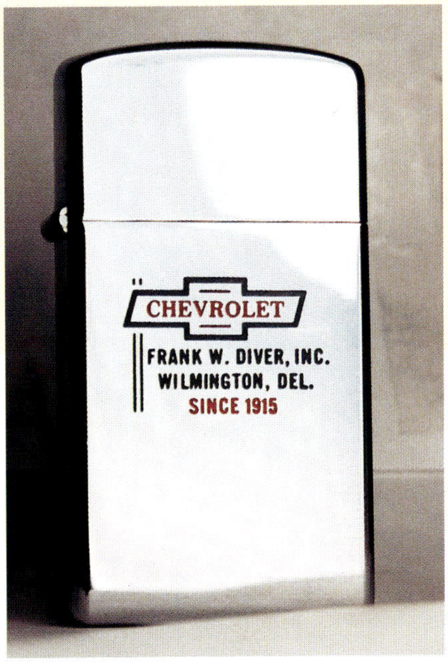

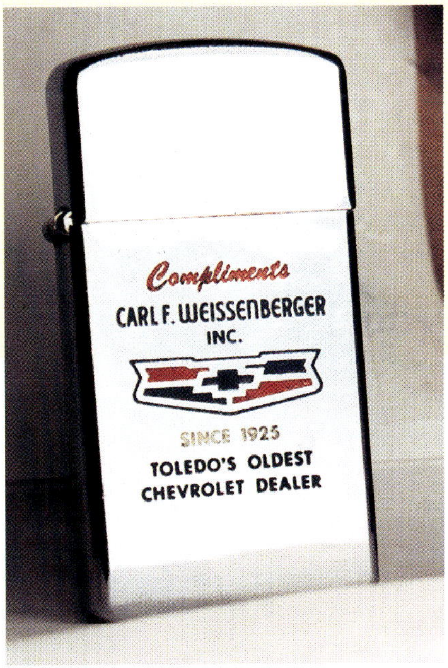

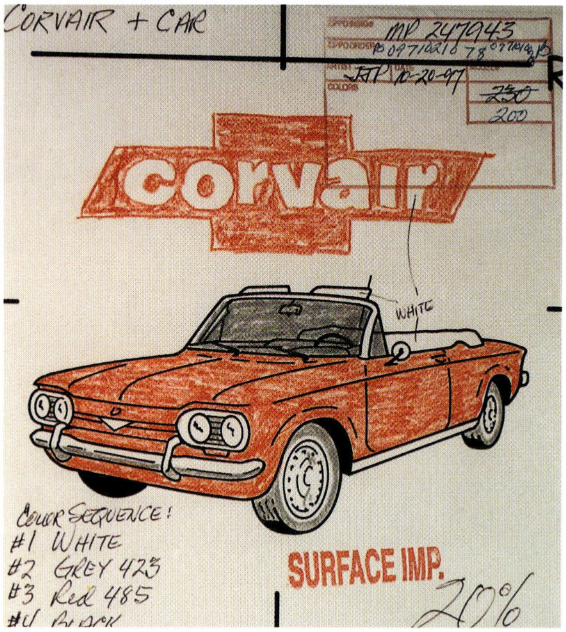

A Corvair lighter and art. This lighter is at Zippo Mfg., and the art was applied to a reproduction square lighter. It is a lovely piece, the only one I have seen. *Courtesy Zippo Mfg.* $40-50

A mint 1991. *Courtesy Parker Collection.* $35-45

A 1957 emblem lighter. *Courtesy Parker Collection.* $75-100

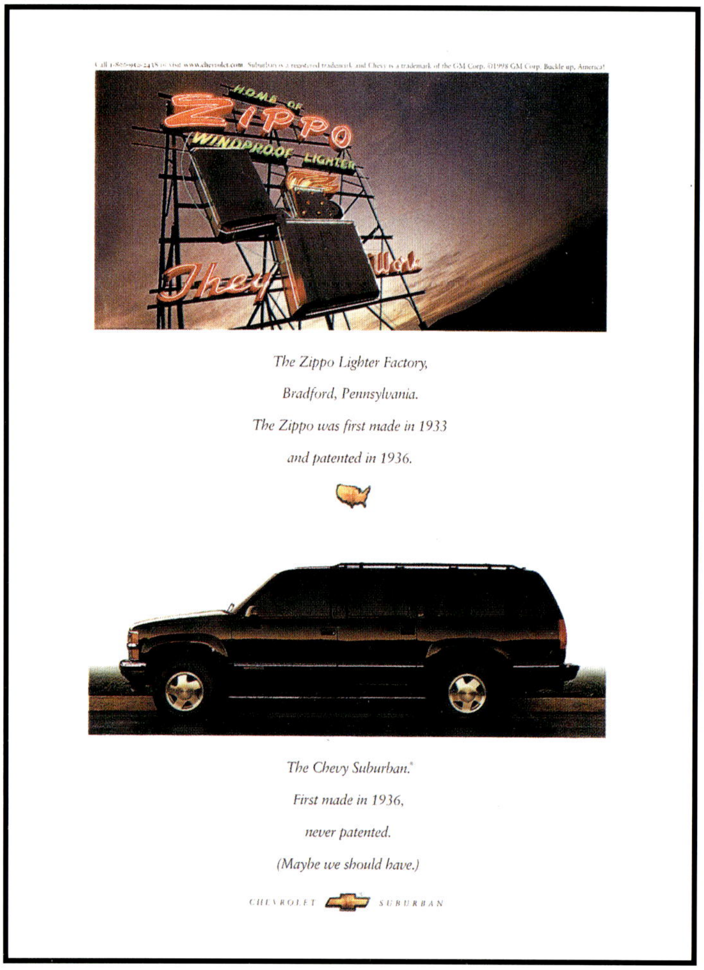

A modern Chevrolet ad with a Zippo Manufacturing connection.

Modern art for the Chevy Cavalier. Zippo lighters are still helping car companies sell cars. *Courtesy Zippo Mfg.*

Pontiac

A very early Pontiac lighter in the Zippo Museum. When this lighter was made, Pontiac was only about a decade old, having become so popular that parent company Oakland was discontinued. $400-600

The Pontiac logo is simple and beautiful. This lighter is from 1953-55. *Courtesy Parker Collection.* $125-150

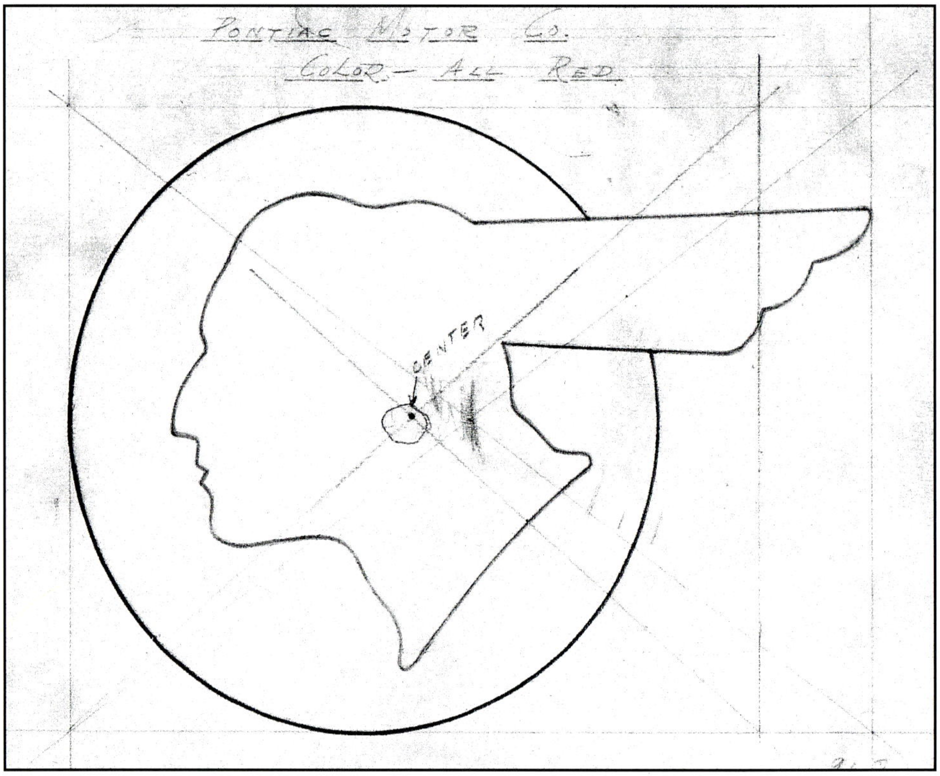

The basic Pontiac Indian head, and a different logo, from 1950.

This emblem, on the other hand, is too small for a full-size lighter. It is legitimate, though. *Courtesy Parker Collection.* $75-100 as is.

Far left: Interesting choice of art, considering the goal is to sell cars. This cardboard dates from June 7, 1954. $40-50 as is.

Left: This lighter's date of 1954 is verified by the cardboard.

Three dealership cardboards. Interestingly, the Morton Pontiac cardboard dates from 1961, though the Arrowhead logo was adopted in 1959. This is probably because the Dealership sign still had the old logo.

This 1964 slim still has the old logo on it. $30-40

Wonderful April 19, 1956 cardboard. I have never seen one of these lighters, but the combination of gold, blue, red, and the detailed picture make it one to search for. This art is based on a Pontiac hood ornament.

This 1968 cardboard shows art that will go onto a gold Barcroft table lighter, as well as regular lighters. Again, the Indian head is still being used, because it is part of the dealership's marquee. Seifert Pontiac is no longer in business, at least by that name.

Three arrowhead lighters. The arrowhead first showed up on Pontiac cars in 1959. $20-30 slim, $75-100 full size

Designs for the Pontiac Sunfire. Note the dates of the artwork.

A Fiero slim from 1986. The Fiero was a huge flop. Both the design and the lighter are simple, but MIB. Owned by the Zippo Museum. $40

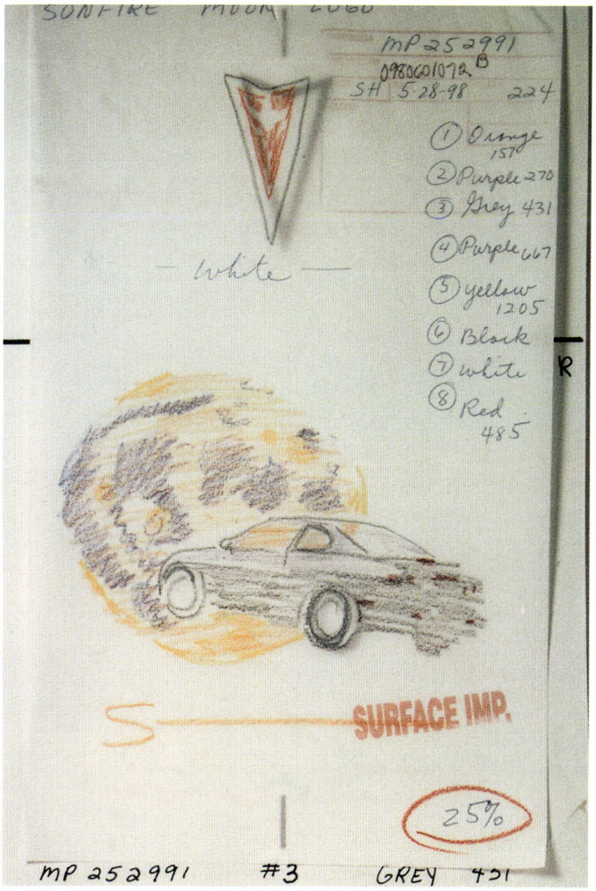

Another Sunfire design, and its result. This lighter is property of Zippo Mfg. $40-50

Artwork for a Zippo lighter series featuring '50s cars. Note the "silver streak" running down the center of the hood, a Pontiac trademark for years.

Buick

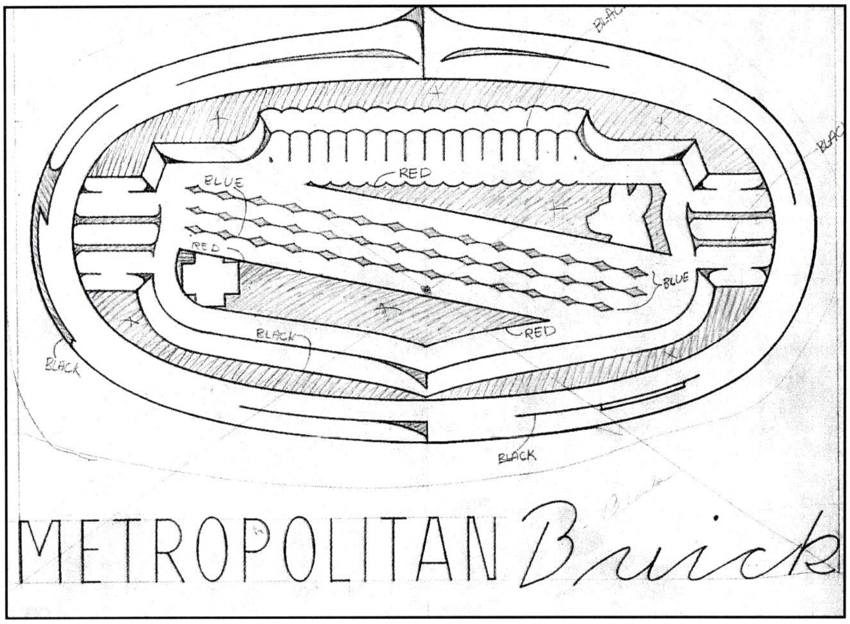

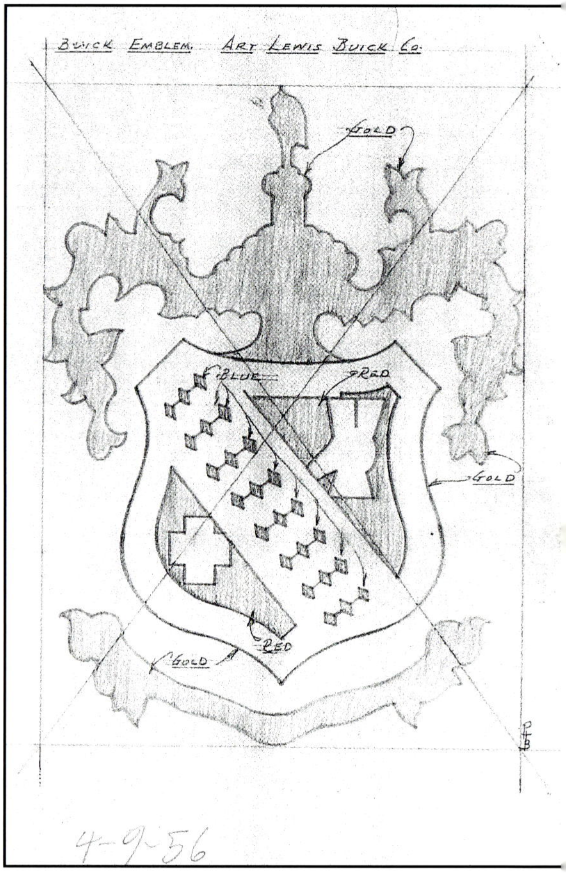

Above and right: Two versions of the Buick crest logo. One of them is a superb cardboard from September 1951.

It is confusing that a lighter would advertise two different dealerships, but this one does. This artwork dates from November 1958.

An early 1950s Buick lighter. This example was probably intended for customers instead of employees. *Courtesy Richard Weinstein.* $150-175

A 1956 Buick Dealership lighter. *Courtesy Parker Collection.* $100-125

A mint 1953-55 lighter with an interesting Buick stamp. $150-175

An anniversary lighter, from 1953, with a #203 bottom stamp. Not mint, but a must for any Buick fan. Note the minute emblem wear at the join of the white to the blue. $150-175

From 1981, "Happy" the hawk. *Courtesy Parker Collection.* $40-50

Three early "tri-shield" lighters. Notice the shield detail. $100-125

Early "tri-shield" slim lighters. Compare with the later version. The emblem lighter is mint, though Zippo didn't do the engraving. $40

The detail was removed from the "tri-shield" by 1964. The new logo is not nearly as pleasing as the original.

Two variations of the Harrison logo. Yellow always stands out on a Zippo lighter. *Courtesy Parker Collection.* Slim, $30-50; full, $60-75

A 1956 Buick dealership cardboard..

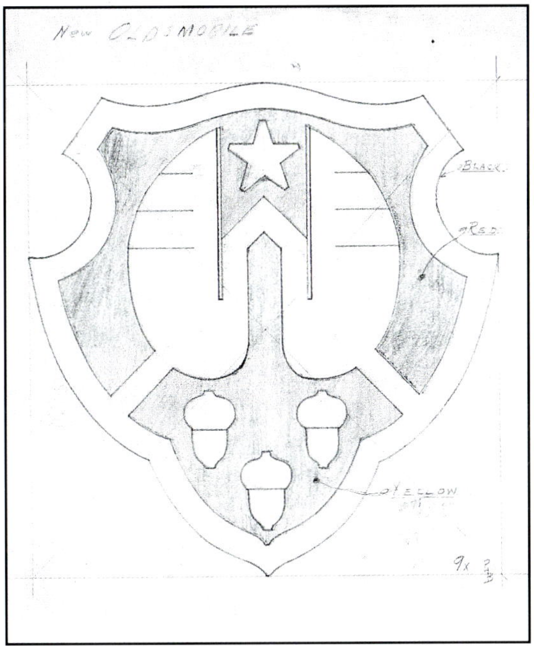

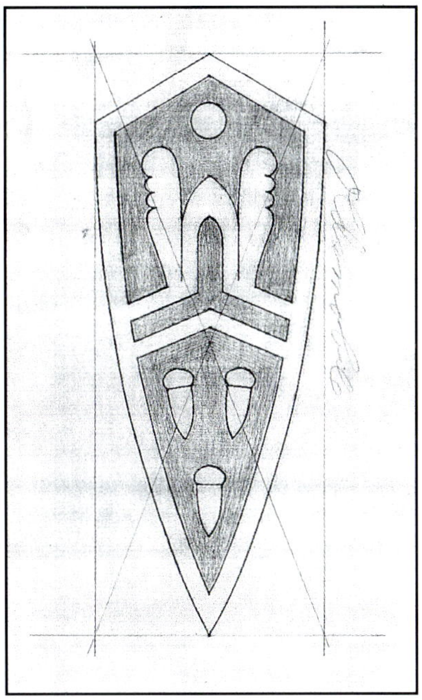

Three undated Cardboards, one of which was redone.

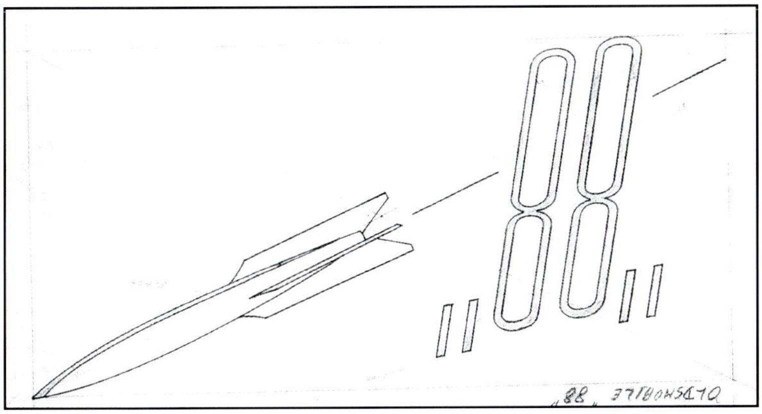

A 1953 cardboard, and a simpler undated version. The "88" and "98" were top-line Oldsmobile cars. The '53 cardboard calls for five colors, including orange. The cardboards in this book give an idea of just how rare the artwork is with more than four colors.

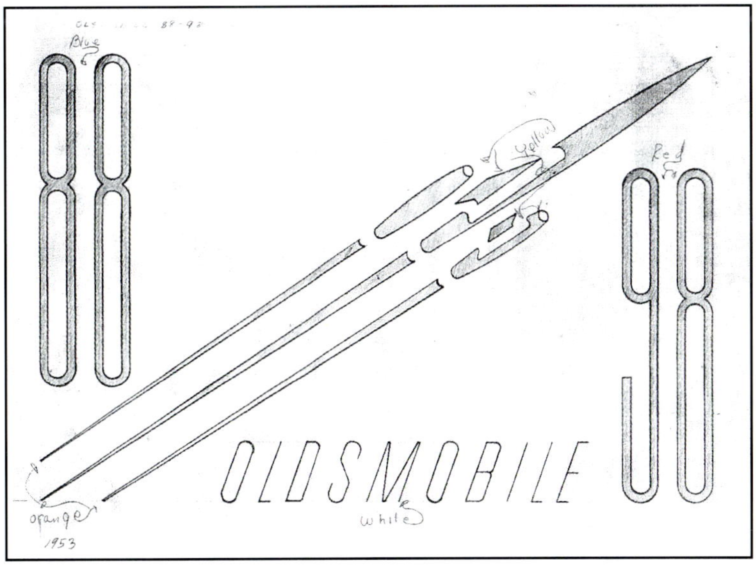

Several dated cardboards. None has more then four colors, but the complexity of the designs makes each of these stunning. Compare the Chevrolet logo to those in the Chevy section.

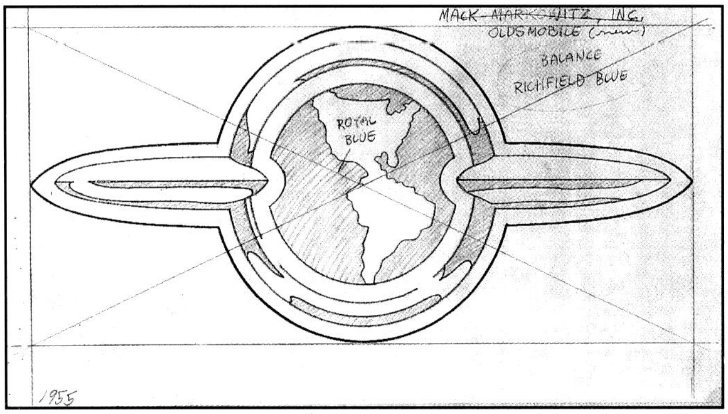

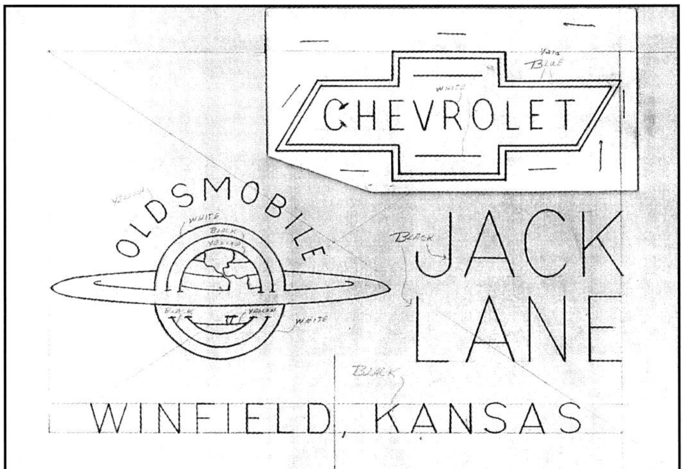

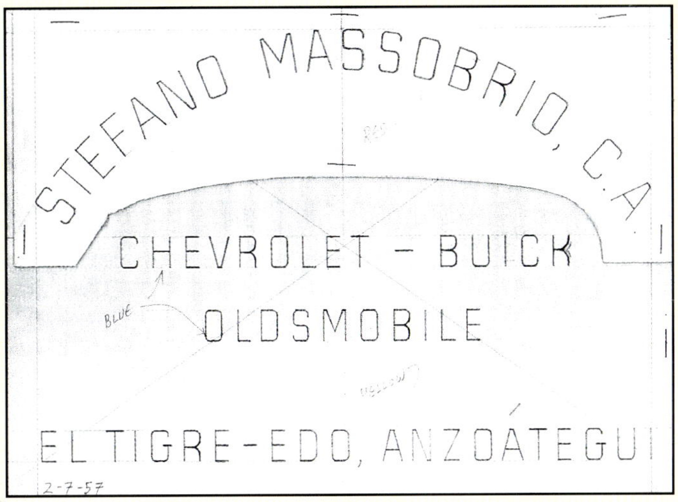

Two text-only cardboards, one from February 7, 1957. Artwork is much more attractive then text alone.

Two simpler cardboards.

Two terrific cardboards. Oldsmobile cardboards are universally beautiful, but the lighters are rare.

A original brass Olds "88" lighter and a 1966 Toronado slim. *Courtesy Richard Weinstein and Parker Sheldon.* $200-250, $40-50 respectively.

A MIB 1963 Olds slim. $30-40

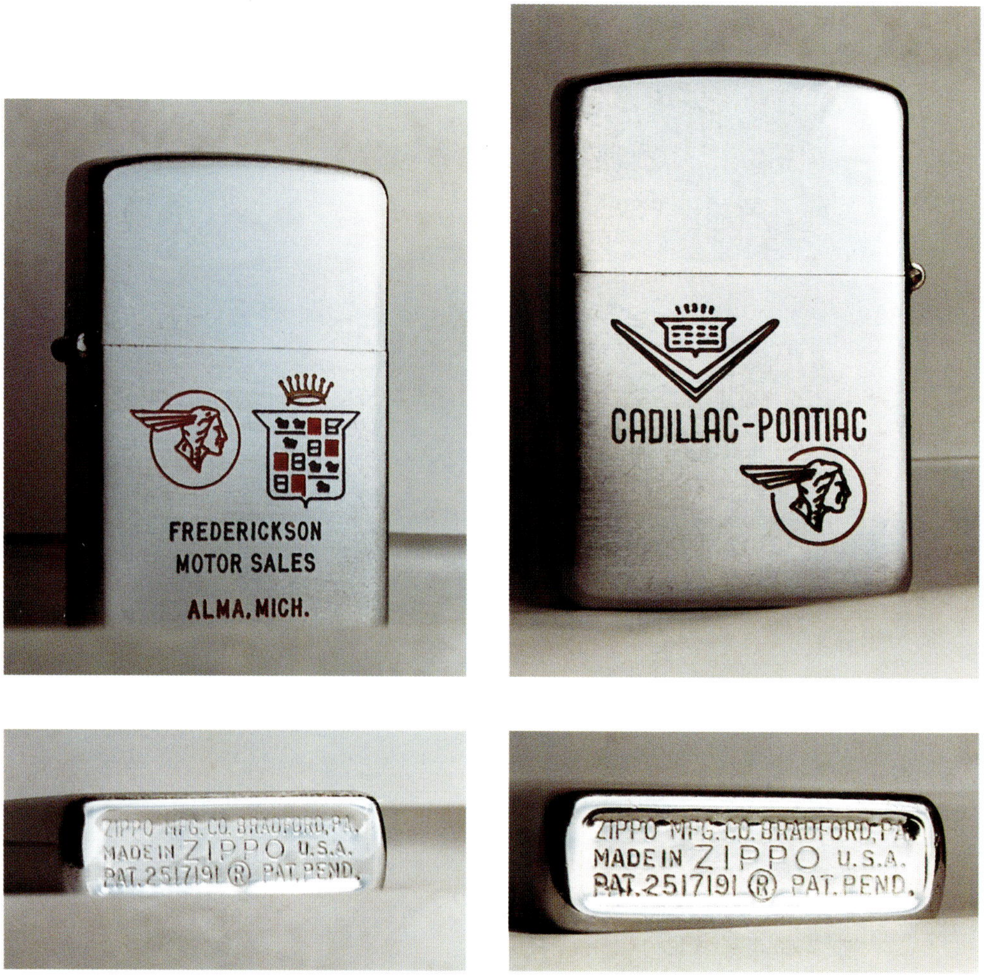

These lighters have the same bottom stamp and the same Pontiac logo. *Courtesy Parker Collection.* $150-175

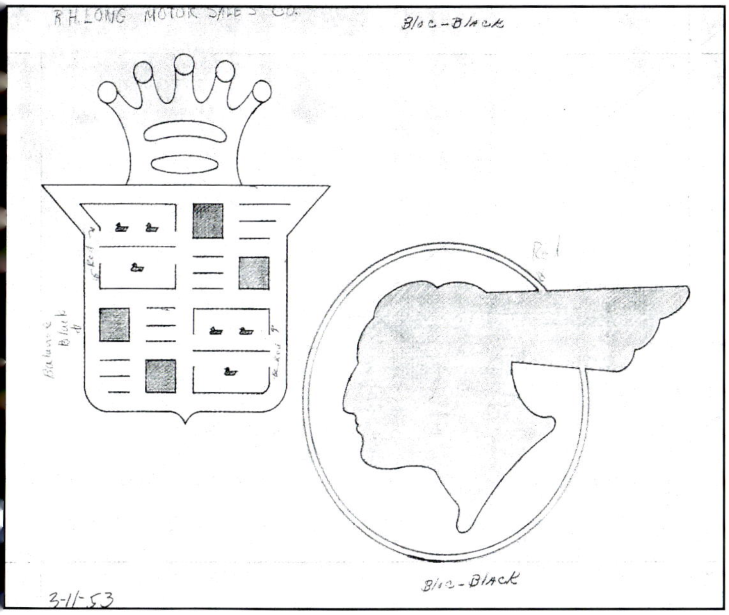

Cadillac dealers often sold Pontiacs as well. Note the subtle change in the Cadillac logo.

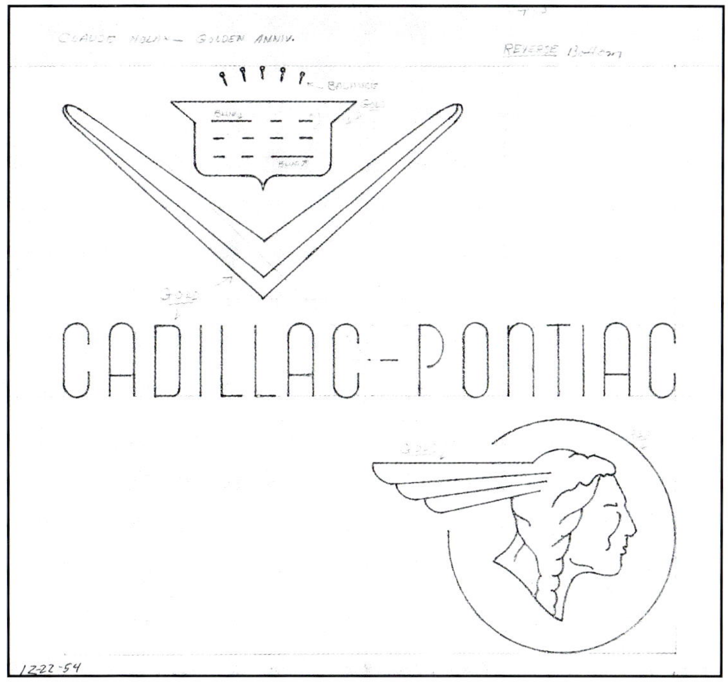

This cardboard obviously dates from 1951. One wonders what kind of cars S&S was selling back in 1876.

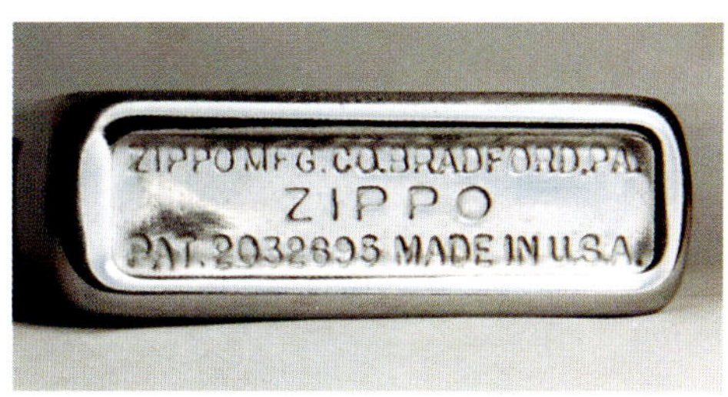

A 1952 Anniversary lighter. Note the beveled five-barrel hinge, and the #203 bottom stamp. *Courtesy Parker Collection.* $125-150

This lighter has a #203 bottom stamp and a three-barrel hinge. Despite the paint loss (about 75% left) this is an attractive lighter. $50-60 as is.

A re-paint would be ill-advised on this three-barrel lighter. Compare with the previous example, which is from the same era. $40-50 as is.

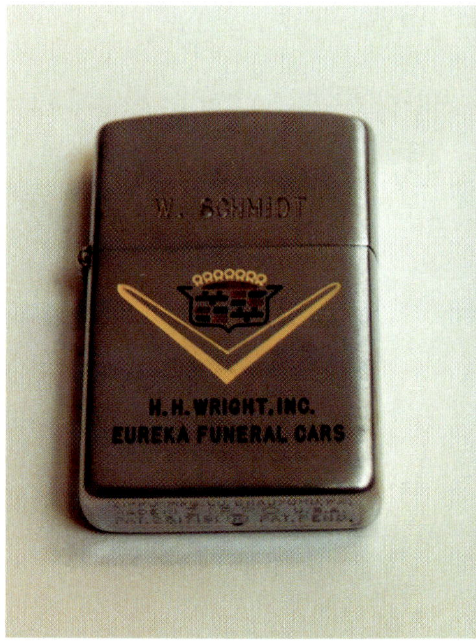

A mint 1954 funeral home lighter, with non-Zippo engraving. *Courtesy Ed Pinedo.* $150-175

Also a 1954, this lighter might be a candidate for a repaint. *Courtesy Parker Collection.* $50-60

This logo is a variation of those on the next page. $45-55

These lighters all have the same logo. Note the year range.

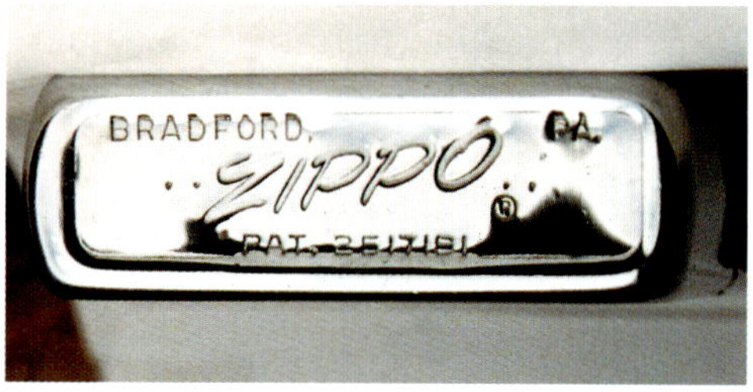

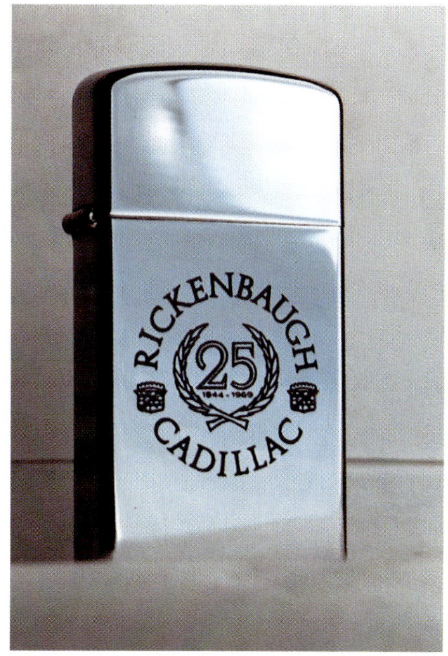

Fourteen years separate these lighters, yet the logo is the same. *Courtesy Parker Collection.* $50-60

Above: A 1969 slim. Note the logo and that the lighter case is from 1968. *Courtesy Parker Collection.* $40-50

A mint 1971 emblem lighter. Compare with the same emblem in the emblem section. *Courtesy Parker Collection.* $50-60

Left: A gold-filled emblem lighter. Gold-filled, gold, and sterling lighters were not usually dated. *Courtesy Parker Collection.* $75-90

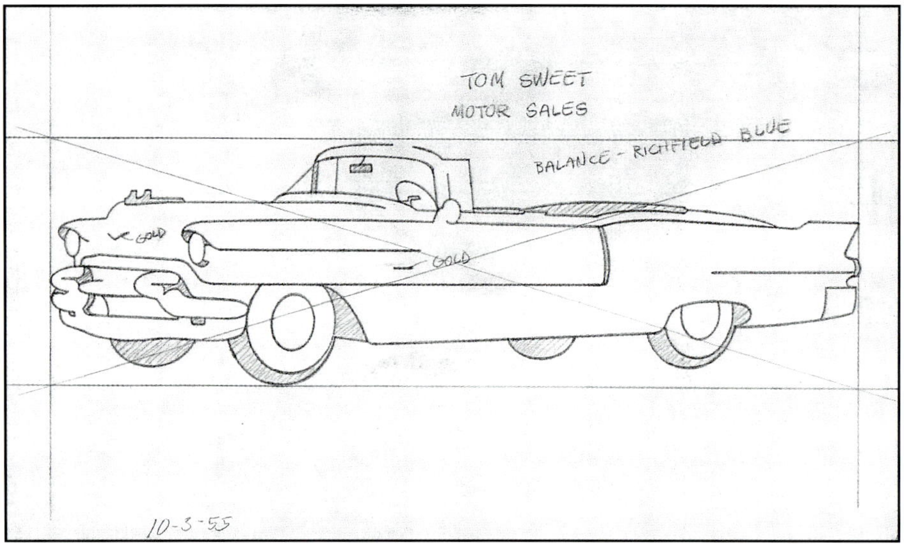

Two cardboards, including a rare and highly detailed auto drawing. Compare the three-color Sunset dealership cardboard with the corresponding lighter in the brassing section. With a cardboard date of April 1950, one wonders whether the lighter originally had a three or five-barrel hinge.

Cadillac made engines for the Stuart light tank in W.W.II, and has been involved with US Army vehicles ever since. This lighter is 100% perfect. The combination of Cadillac and tank is quite an oxymoron. *Courtesy Mike Meuhlberger.* $300-325

The Commando armored car was made for export. An earlier version had a different Stoner weapons system on the reverse of the lighter. The "X" refers to experimental. *Courtesy Parker Collection.* $150-175

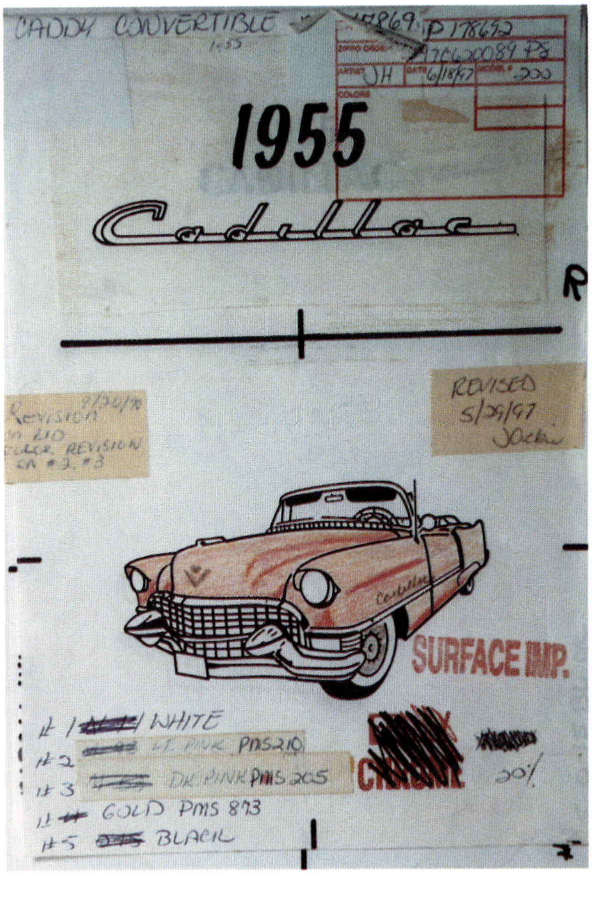

Modern Cadillac art.

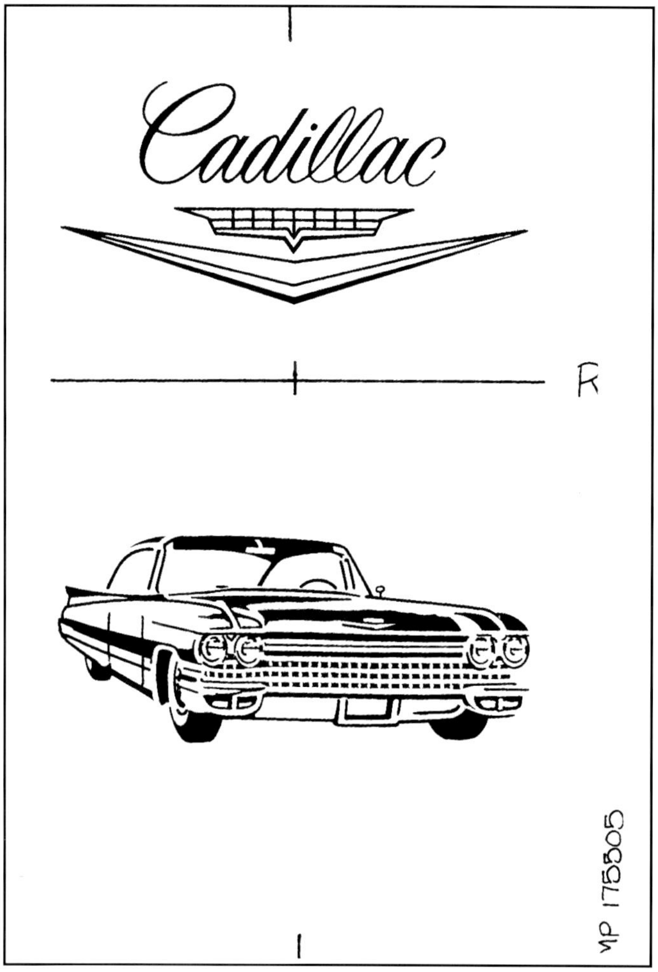

This is luster etch artwork.

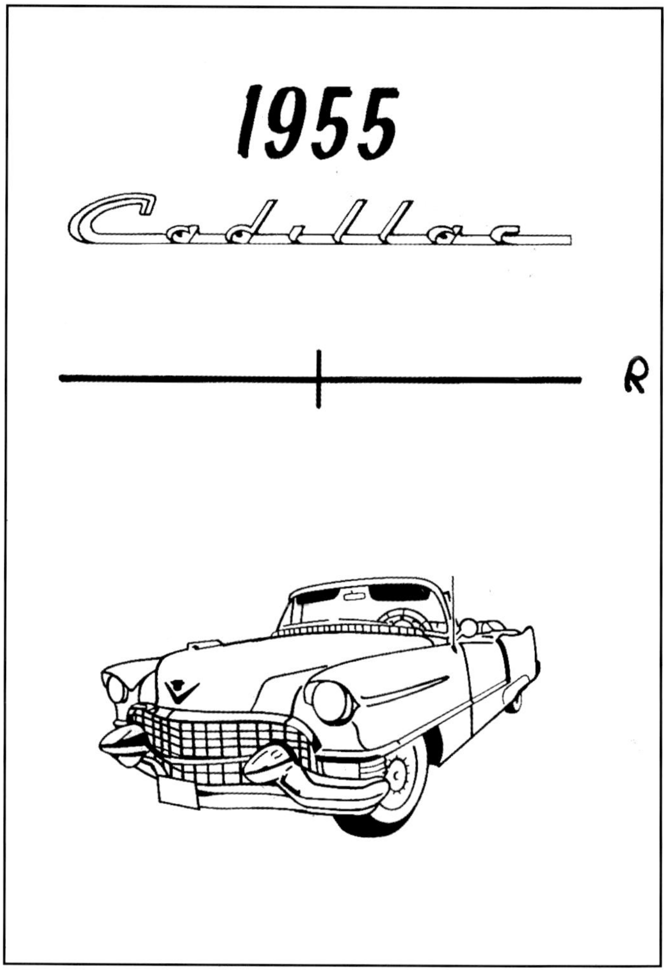

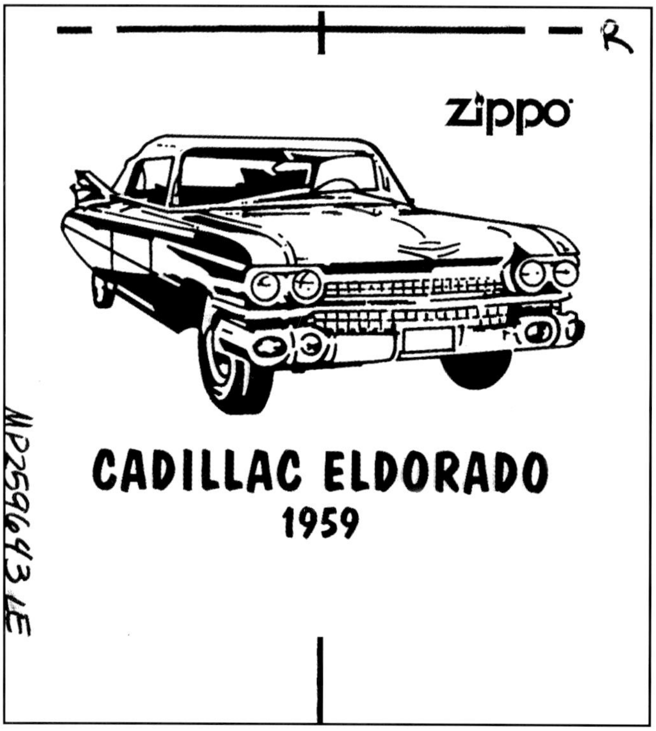

An early '50s GMC blotter, a 1956 GMC cardboard and a #203 five barrel lighter, all with the same logo. $80-90

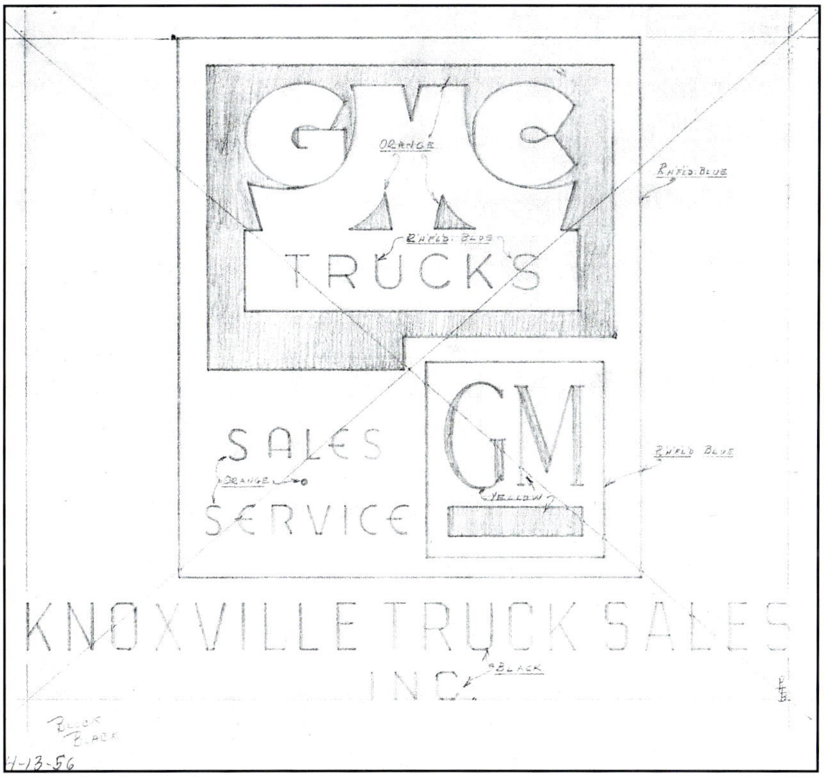

A 1958 lighter from the same dealership, with perhaps 88% paint. $70-80

Mint GMC slims. Polished chrome lighters scratch *extremely* easily, and mint examples are hard to find. *Courtesy Parker Collection.* $30-40

Ford

Above: A Ford Lincoln Zephyr metallique lighter from 1938. This is the most valuable lighter pictured in this book. *Courtesy Richard Weinstein.* $1200-1500

Right: An undated Ford cardboard.

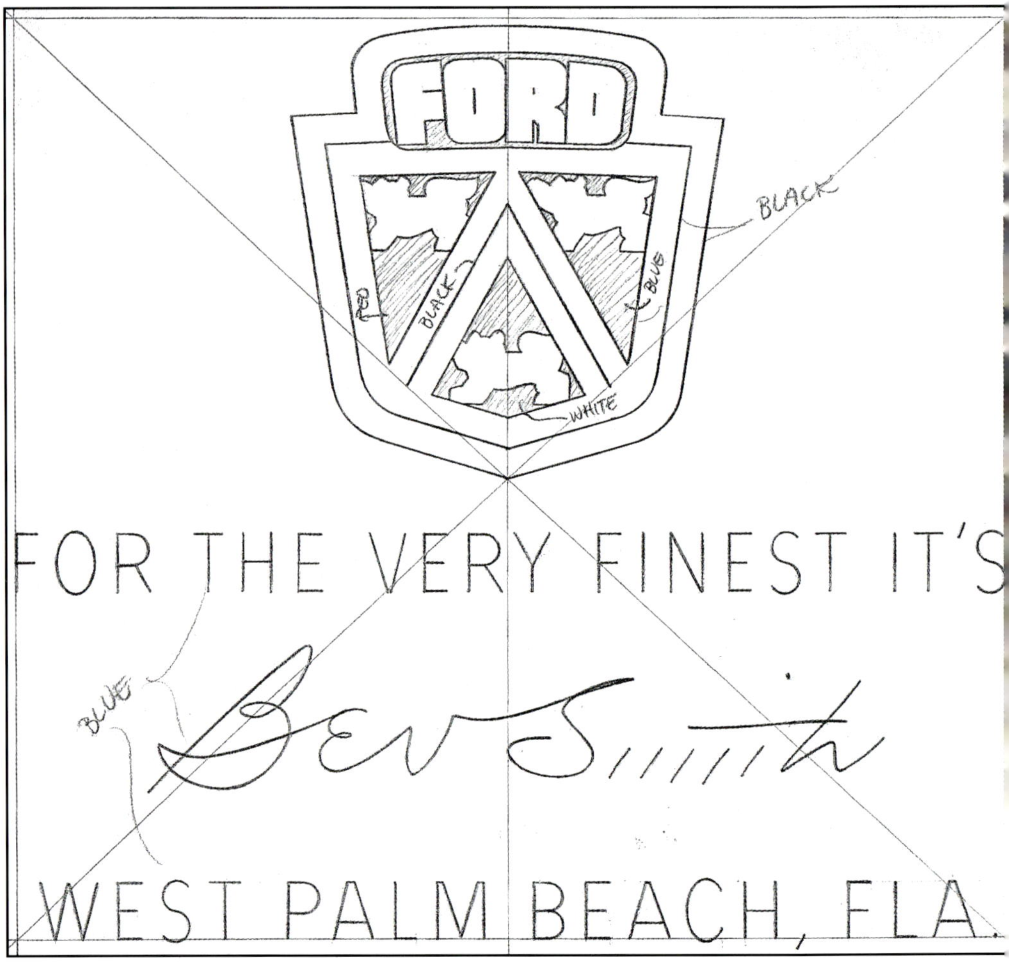

An early and interesting #203 "loss-proof" lighter with the Ford logo on the reverse. Loss-proof lighters had a loop hinge with a lanyard on it. This lighter is missing the lanyard. *Courtesy Ed Pinedo.*

A marvelous #251 Ford anniversary lighter. It should be MIB, but has a frozen flint wheel. $225-250

Henry, Edsel, and Henry II adorn this MIB anniversary lighter. Note the date on the back. The artwork on which this image was based was produced by Norman Rockwell. This lighter also has the #251 full stamp. *Courtesy Parker Collection.* $300-350

A #203 lighter with a five barrel hinge. *Courtesy Parker Collection.*

A #251 full stamp. *Courtesy Parker Collection.*

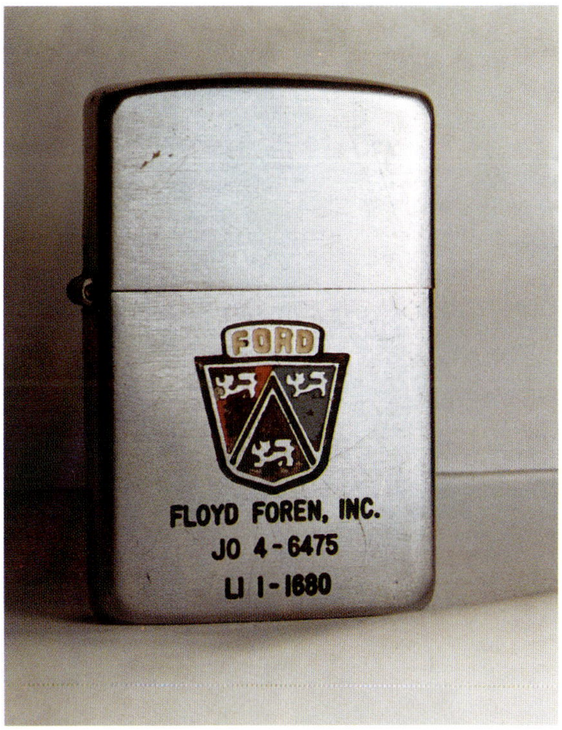

#203 lighters. *Courtesy Parker Collection.*

Lighters from 1958-59. *Courtesy Parker Collection.*

Two 1963 lighters. The text is in blue, a nice touch. Note the difference in condition. *Courtesy Parker Collection.*

Mint 1954 full-stamp #251 lighter. The gold color is actually a clear lacquer, which makes the brass underneath sparkle like gold.

Also a #251 full-stamp. The marring on the front is a shame. *Courtesy Parker Collection.*

Same era and stamp, but compare the condition. *Courtesy Parker Collection.*

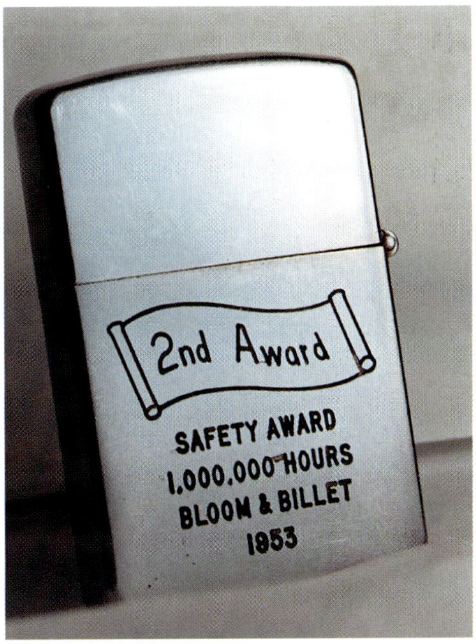

Despite minor brassing on the reverse, this lighter could be re-painted. *Courtesy Parker Collection.*

Note the difference between the condition of these 1962 slims. Mint means a lot. *Courtesy Parker Collection.*

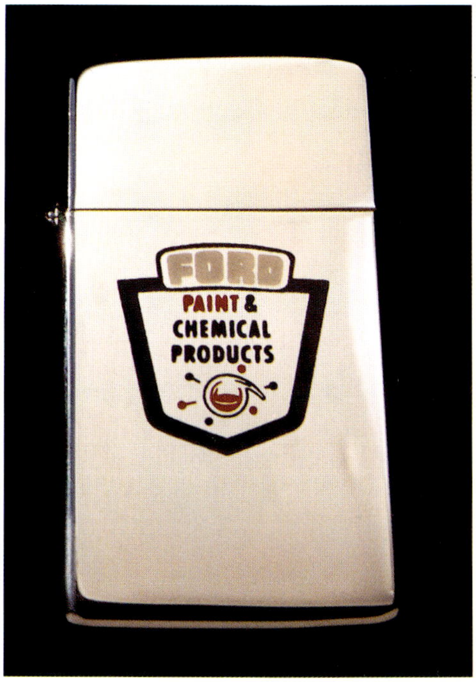

The red, white and blue colors, combined with the perfect chrome and the interesting logo, make this Ford slim stunning.

This 1965 lighter has the Mustang logo on it. Despite the thinness of the chrome, this lighter would benefit from a re-paint. $40-50

A mint Thunderbird slim. *Courtesy Parker Collection.*

At first glance, these lighters are the same, but the 1960 lighter doesn't have the Mustang logo present on the 1965. *Courtesy Parker Collection.*

Though these #203 lighters are text-only, the combination of different scripts and the blue in the logo increase interest.

A complex five-color cardboard from July of an unknown year.

A series of Lincoln-Mercury cardboards. They are all colorful and lovely. The Mercury logo is one of the nicest car logos ever designed.

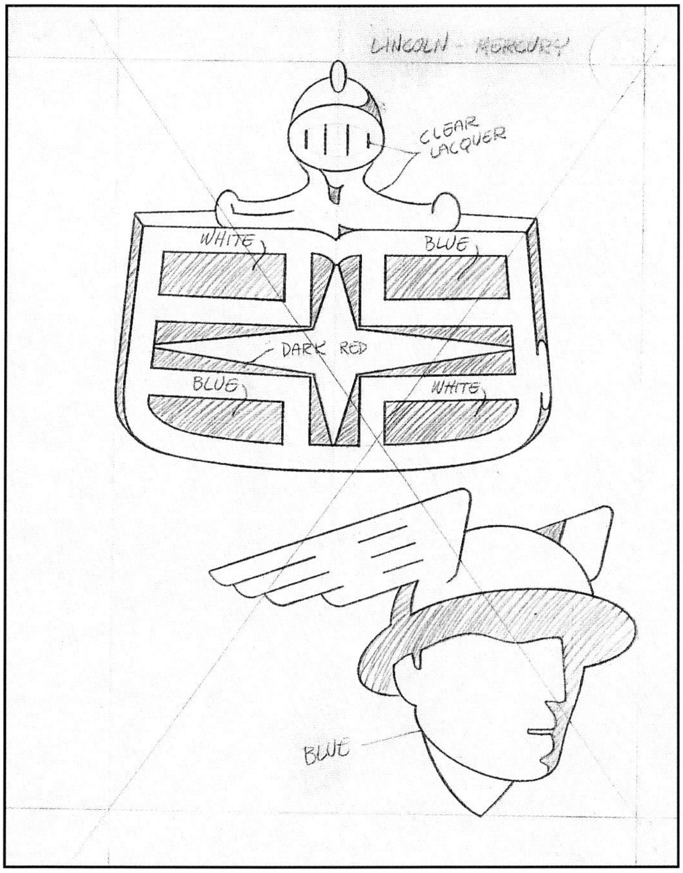

Two 1954 cardboards. These lighters were destined for employees.

Compare the original lighter of a later date (the example with only two logos) with the owner-repainted model (including the Ford logo).

Two Mercury lighters. The Meteor lighter is from Canada.

This #251 full-stamp lighter has a rather badly done non-Zippo engraving on the reverse. This is still a complex and colorful lighter.

Two Lincoln-Mercury cardboards.

A Lincoln cardboard and a lighter based on it. Dealers who sold only Lincolns were uncommon. *Courtesy Richard Weinstein.*

A 1963 Continental emblem lighter. *Courtesy Parker Collection.* $50-75

Two Lincoln cardboards, and the new Continental logo. This 1964 cardboard indicates that the same logo will go on both full-size and slim lighters.

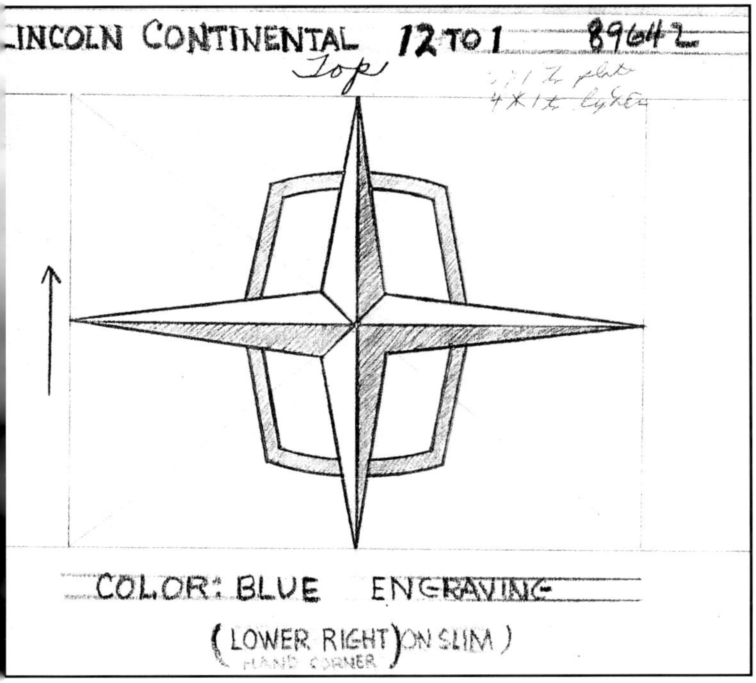

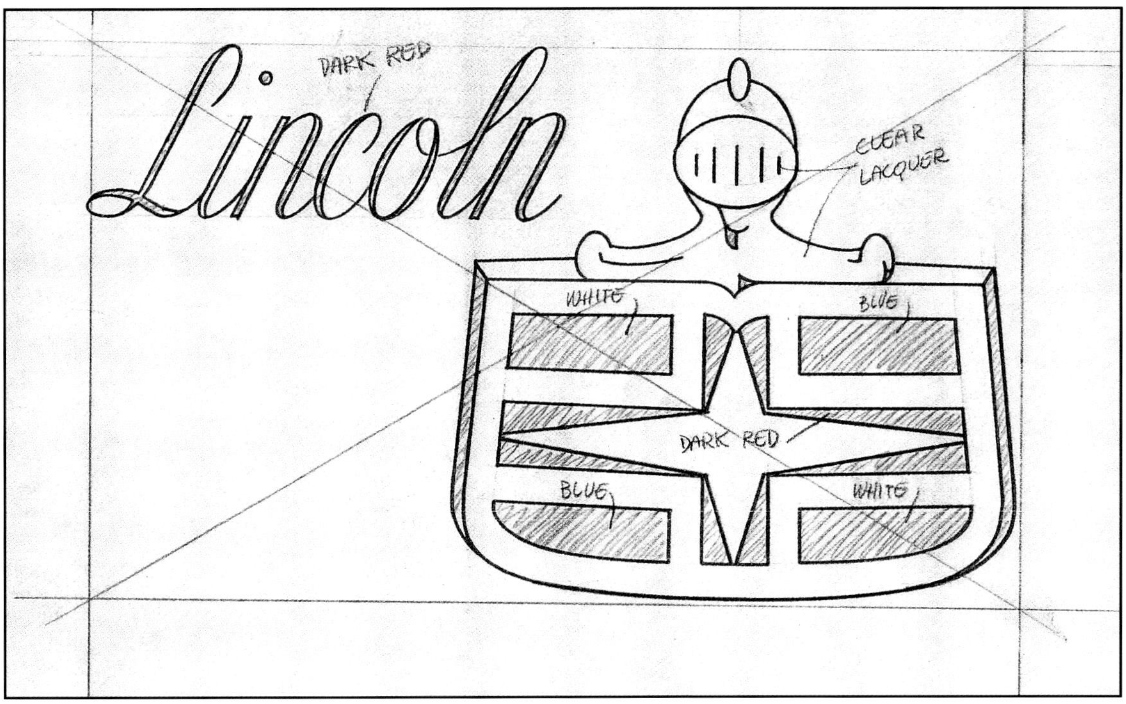

Four "in-house" lighters. Note the different logos. *Courtesy Parker Collection.*

A rather mundane cardboard with the single color, black. Notice that, though the artwork is for 1969, the cardboard itself is dated October 1968.

Gotta have an Edsel lighter in here somewhere. The lighter has been owner-repainted; but even so, it is one of the most sought-after bits of auto memorabilia. Compare it with the original dealer label. *Courtesy Parker Collection.* $300-350 as is.

This is a MIB Edsel lighter. *Courtesy of Ed Pinedo* $400-450

Four highly detailed pieces of art for various series of commemorative lighters.

1975. The signature was probably that of an employee. This lighter is unused, but has scratches on the case. $40-50 as is.

A Zippo Manufacturing ad for commemorative Mustang lighters.

Two commemorative series lighters. $30-40 if not part of a full set.

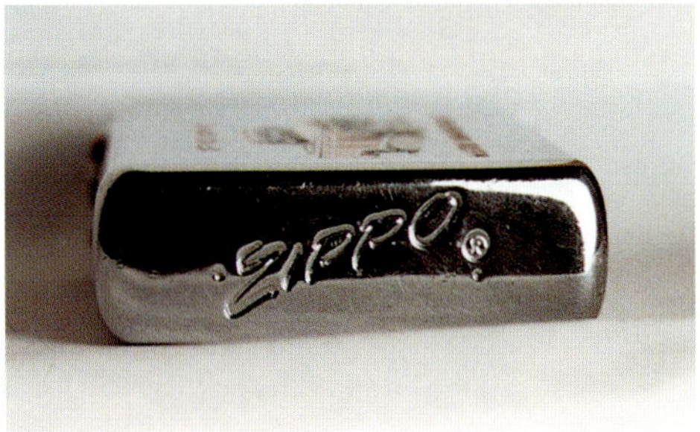

A modern Ford truck Zippo lighter. $30-40

A Ford slim from 1963. The truck detail is striking. $30-40 as is.

A Ford truck emblem slim. Note the 1960 inscription on a 1959 slim lighter. The slim date codes were one "dot" behind the full-size lighters until 1966, after which the code was the same for both sizes. *Courtesy Parker Collection.* $20-30

Chrysler

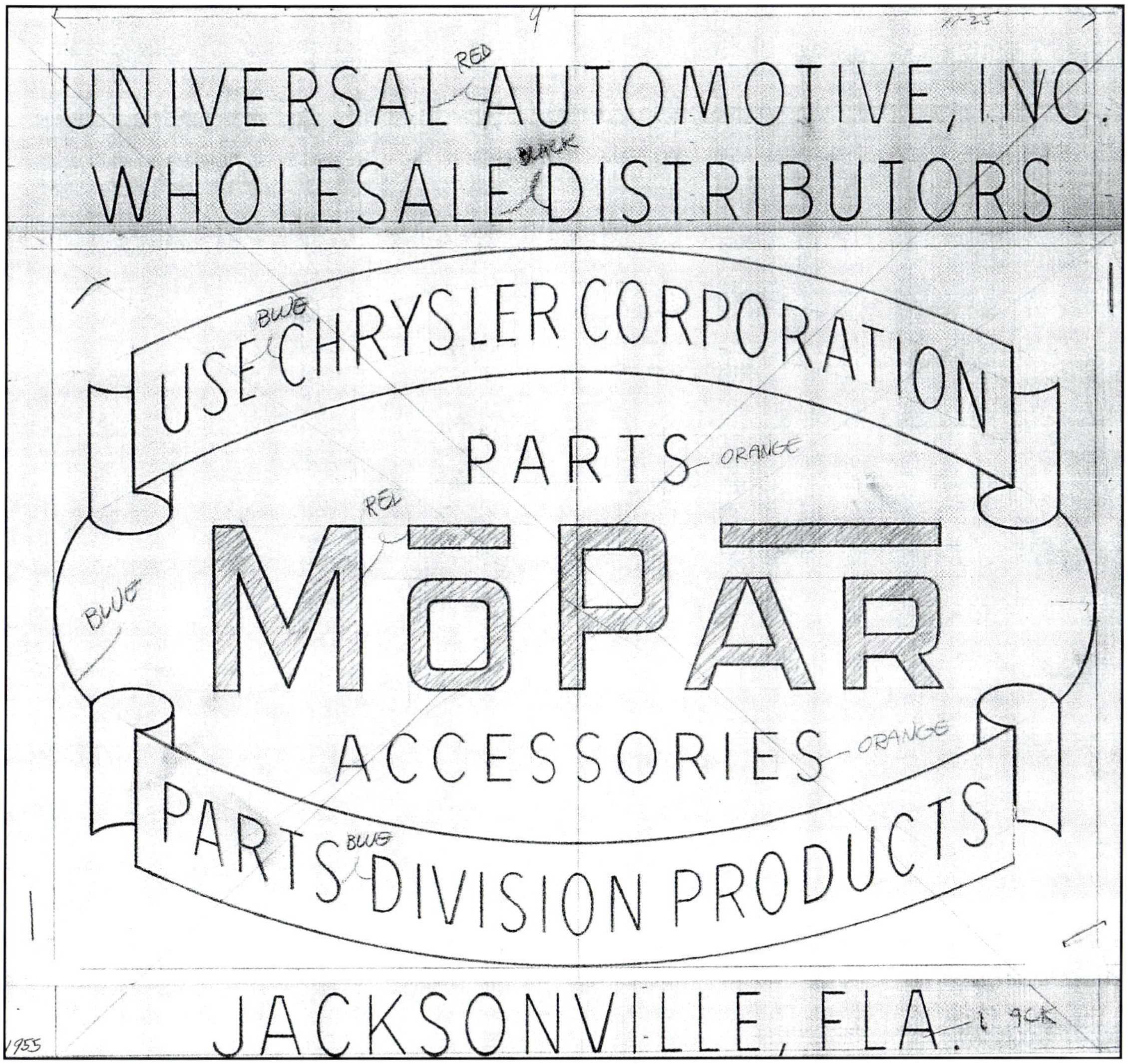

Three variations of the same logo, including one in French. A translation appears to be, "Use the pieces of the Chrysler Corporation." Probably sounds better in French. This art was destined for Quebec, rather than for France. Note the colors and the dates, and that two cardboards have no color indication.

A #203 lighter, with 98% paint. This lighter was made before mid-1953. The colors are different from those indicated by the cardboard, but this lighter is definitely genuine. *Courtesy Parker Collection.* $150-175

A MIB #251 lighter. The box has the same name as is inscribed on the back. There is minor red overspray in the white text and lid areas, which does not alter the beauty of this lighter one whit. The red is especially noticeable. $150-175

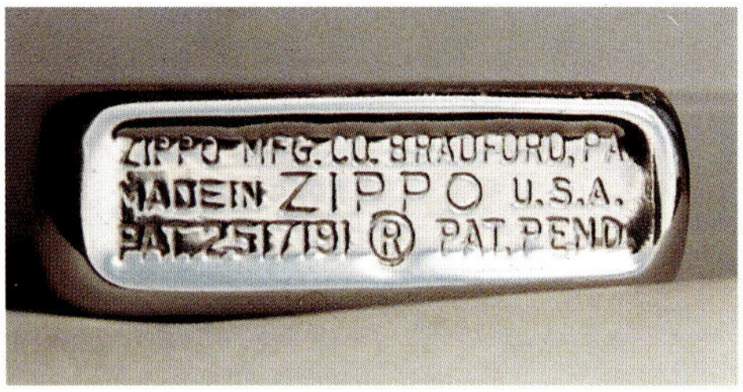

Another #251 lighter. The paint, though 100%, has faded slightly. *Courtesy Parker Collection.* $125-150

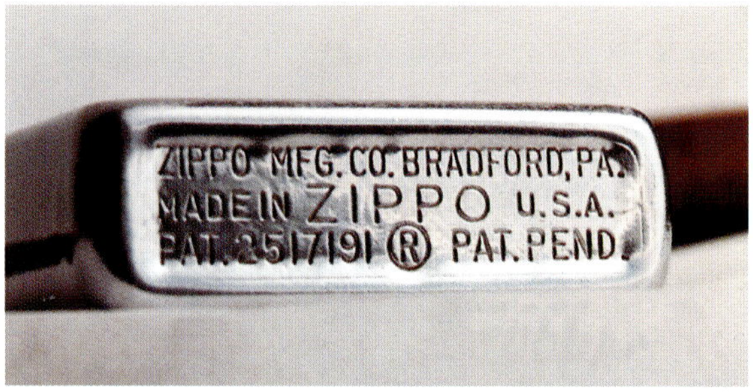

This #251 lighter has been rather savagely re-hinged. There is about 60% paint. All these Chrysler lighters are genuine and original. *Courtesy Parker Collection.* $50-75 as is.

A mint 1957 "master technician conference" lighter. $130-150

Chrysler's "master technician." This little figure adorned mechanic lighters and service awards for several years. Notice the 1955 date on the seven-year pin.

A #251 "conference leader" lighter. The red on the reverse is the same shade and thickness as the previous "Mopar" lighters. This variation of the "master technician" lighter is uncommon. *Courtesy Parker Collection.* $150-175

A #203 five-barrel Chrysler "rosette" lighter. The red in this lighter is darker than in the previous lighters.

This lighter has the first "dot" stamp on it but is valued in the #251 "era." There are eight dots; PAT. 2517191 is on the left, and PAT. PEND is on the right. The high-quality engraving is not by Zippo. Notice the red color. This is a late 1955 lighter. $150-175

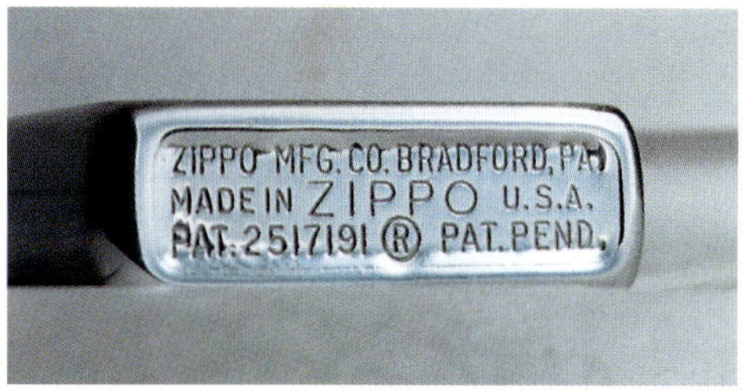

This beautiful 1956 advertising lighter has the #251 full stamp. The inscription (by Zippo) means it was not a prototype. It was probably ordered very early in calendar year 1955, before the "dot" stamp came out. The previous lighter has the exact same logo and a 1955 inscription on the back—yet has the *later* bottom stamp. *Courtesy Parker Collection.* $150-175

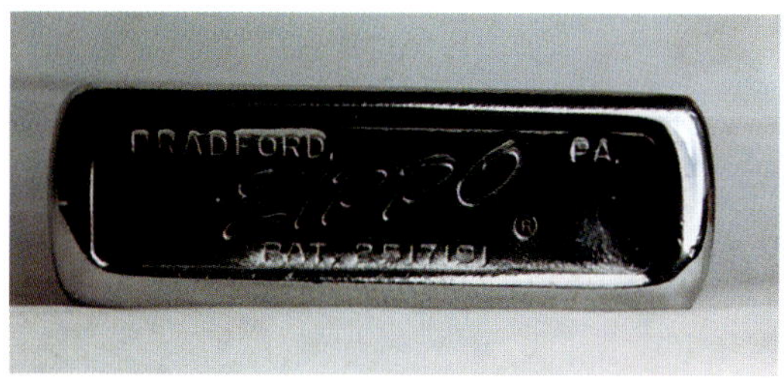

Chrysler began using the pentastar logo in 1962. This mint, but rather plain, 1964 lighter is an early example. The paint is black, instead of blue. *Courtesy Parker Collection.* $100-125

Two pentastar logo lighters. $75-100

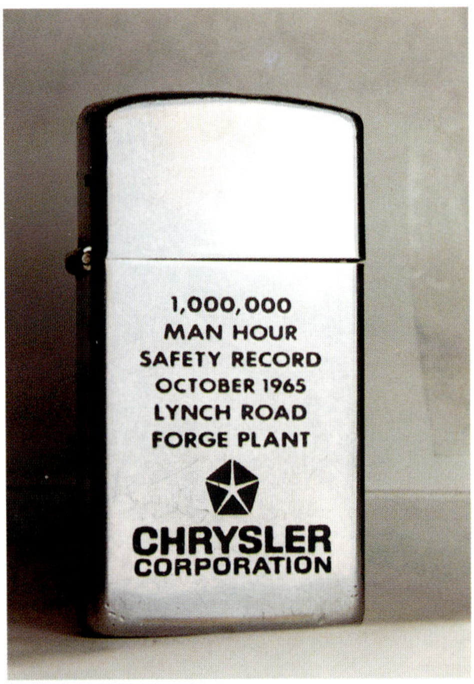

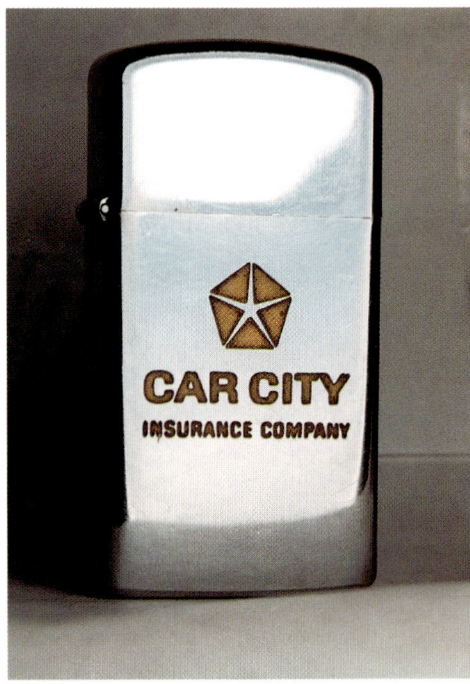

Three pentastar slims. Compare to the rosette logo. *Courtesy Parker Collection.* $30-40

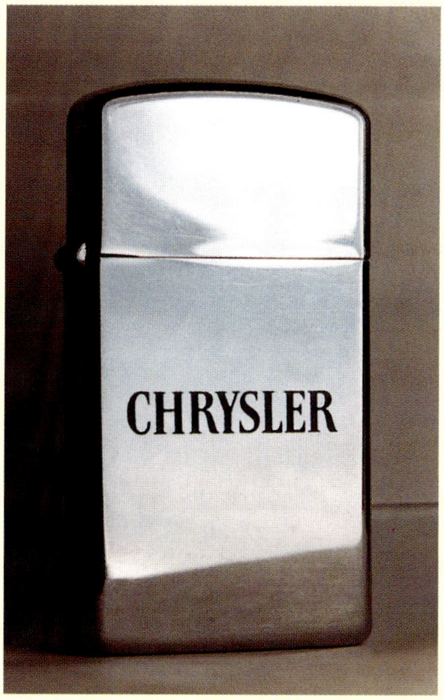

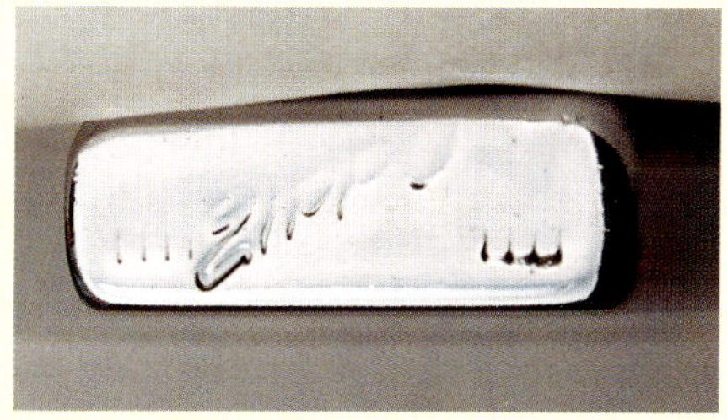

This mint 1966 lighter is an example of the least desirable advertising lighter: a block letter, text-only slim. Note the weak bottom strike. *Courtesy Parker Collection.* $50-60

A logo-only lighter with a rosette in the center. Despite zero paint, and thinning of the chrome, this lighter is nicer then the previous one. *Courtesy Parker Collection.* $50-60 as is.

A MIB three-barrel DeSoto lighter. *Courtesy Michael Gover.* This lighter sold for $300.

All these DeSoto lighters have 3-barrel hinges and originally had blue paint. C*ourtesy Parker Collection, Ed Pinedo, Michael Gover.*

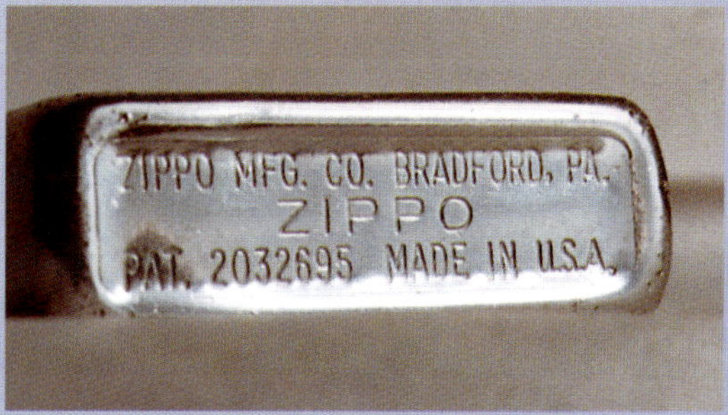

A different logo DeSoto lighter.
Courtesy Parker Collection.

A plain 1957 cardboard.

A 1954 Dodge cardboard, and a 1952 five-color Dodge-Plymouth Dealership cardboard.

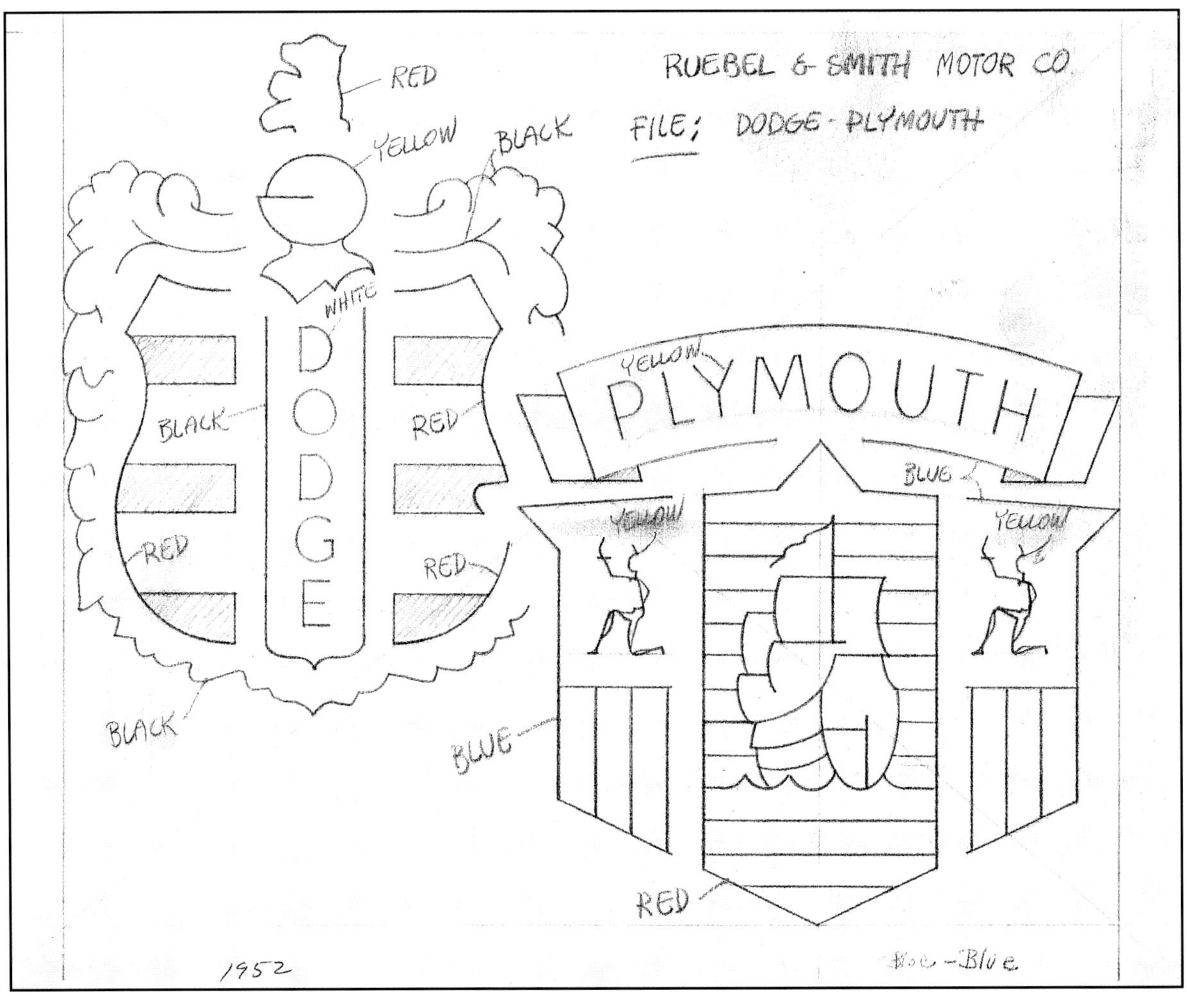

Two Dodge-Plymouth dealership cardboards. I do not know what "Pa color" refers to. Possibly, the ordering dealership hadn't decided on the final color scheme for the artwork.

A new appreciation for the beauty of a complex, five-color design. $80-100

A plain Dodge lighter from 1969, with simple black text. *Courtesy Parker Collection.* $40-50

This three-barrel lighter has lid engraving, two types of script, and two shades of red, in addition to the green of the main text. $60-80 as is.

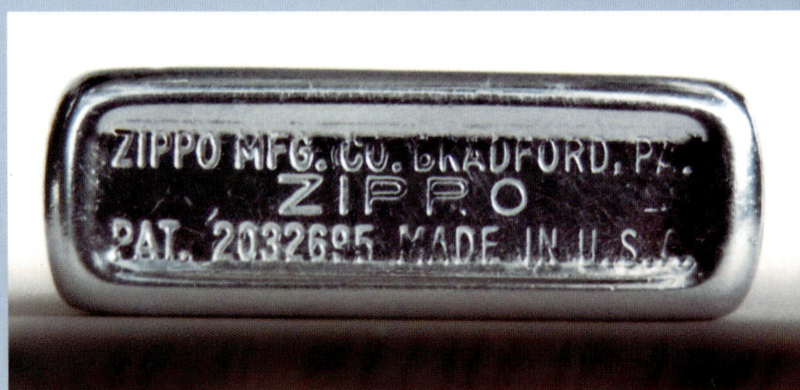

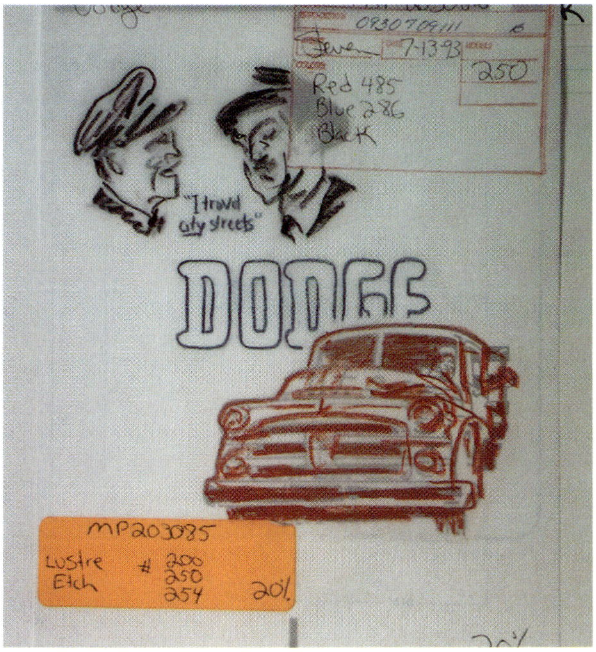

Modern art for Dodge trucks.

A new ad campaign. The lighter dates from 1966. The rule can be dated to the same era. *Rule courtesy Michael Gover, lighter Courtesy Parker Collection.* Rule: $30-40; lighter: $50-75.

Two Plymouth Roadrunner lighters. Despite the wear, these are both worth a lot. *Courtesy Parker Collection.* $200-250 as is.

Plymouth paid Warner Brothers $50,000 for the rights to the Roadrunner name. Allegedly, Plymouth did not have the right to put the Roadrunner logo on secondary items like lighters, and lighter production was stopped. If true, it would explain why mint examples fetch up to $300. A Roadrunner Zippo knife can bring $275. Note the Roadrunner logo on the air-cleaner of this 1969 Roadrunner. *Courtesy Ron Goudreau and Parker Collection.*

A 1969 Plymouth ad campaign slim. It is mint, and strikingly colorful. Even though it is a slim, it is worth $75-100.

A 1951 Jeep cardboard. No colors are indicated, though the detail is impressive. This is actually a Willys Jeep advertisement.

By 1957, when this three-color cardboard was done, Jeep was owned by Kaiser, which had ceased making passenger cars in the US. AMC bought Jeep in 1970.

Two pieces of recent Jeep art. Chrysler bought AMC, and Jeep, in 1987. The last AMC car was built December 14, 1987.

A midnight chrome lighter with a tin and a Jeep display panel. This panel is a generic one. Cardboard inserts announcing a particular series are used to identify the particular lighters being displayed. Compare this panel with the Corvette display. Jeep is now owned by Daimler-Chrysler. MIB (**M**int **I**n **B**ox) Chrysler Jeep lighters: $25-30.

Two 1964 three-color Cummins diesel lighters.

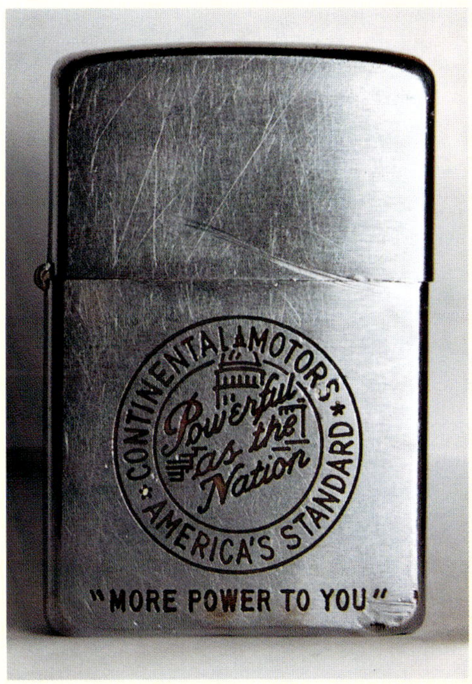

Continental engines powered everything from Kaiser-Frazers to Jeeps. They also were used in Stuart light tanks during W.W.II, until Cadillac engines replaced them. A very old company, there is a Continental metallique in the Zippo Museum. These lighters are both #203 five-barrels. $100-125

Two Holley lighters. The tired one is a #203 five-barrel; the other is a mint 1975 lighter. #203 lighter: $40-50; mint lighter: $50-60.

Two Radiator shop lighters. The slightly used left example is from 1958. The other is mint and dates from 1961. Note the subtle differences between the two logos. Each of these lighters would fetch $60-75.

Both Borg-Warner and Pittsburgh Plate Glass are part of Daimler-Chrysler. The Borg-Warner lighter is mint while the Pittsburgh Plate Glass model is a well-done Zippo re-paint. Borg-Warner lighter: $75-100; Pittsburgh Plate Glass lighter: $40-50.

Epilogue

As I write this, the 21st century is but days away. In the last hundred years, the auto has grown from its humble beginnings as a plaything of the wealthy to become the single most important product owned by the households of the world. Modern cars have amenities and abilities beyond comprehension by the auto pioneers. They are all superb vehicles ... and yet, they lack something.

Individuality, perhaps—they all look alike, all rounded bubbles, perfect for those who wish to go from A to B, possibly, but difficult to find in a full parking lot. All are cars that seem to have come from one collective mind, with only one approach to doing things.

The independents are all gone, and with them went ways of thinking that can never be recovered. The large corporations, too, have lost much of the individuality that once set apart divisions and corporations. This fact is one reason, at least, that Chrysler is discontinuing Plymouth after the 2000 model year. Yet, as long as there are people who honor the past, who appreciate car engineers and designers who thought differently from their brethren, there will be a desire for the big, unique cars from the beginning of the American automobile experience. That desire will never fade.

Zippo lighters will be there as well, creating the wind-proof flame. Fewer people are smoking these days, but there has always been fire, the most basic tool in human experience. Since 1933, Zippo lighters have supplied fire, in a little hand-held container, two inches by two ounces, copied, but never equaled.

That fire will never go out.

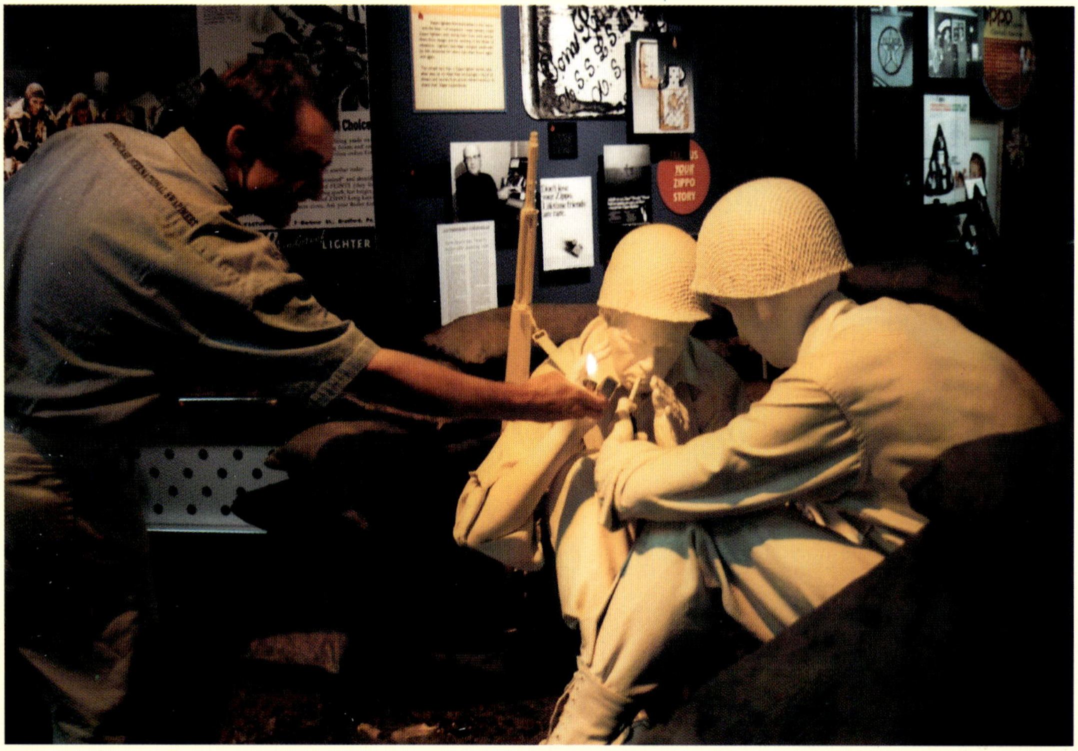

At the Zippo Museum, July 1999.

Bibliography

Imai, Kesaharu. *Zippo Manual*, Vols 1-4. Tokyo, Japan: World Photo Press, 1992.

Rae, John B. *The American Automobile.* Chicago, Ill & London, England: The University Of Chicago Press, 1965.

Pearson, Charles T. *The Indomitable Tin Goose.* New York, New York: Abelard-Schuman Ltd., 1960. Reprinted by Motorbooks International, Minneapolis, Minnesota.

Langworth, Richard M. *Hudson: The Postwar Years.* Osceola, Wisconsin: Motorbooks International Publishers & Wholesalers, Inc., 1977.

Langworth, Richard M. *Illustrated Studebaker Buyer's Guide.* Osceola, Wisconsin: Motorbooks International Publishers & Wholesalers, Inc., 1991.

Langworth, Richard M. *Illustrated Packard Buyer's Guide.* Osceola, Wisconsin: Motorbooks International Publishers & Wholesalers, Inc., 1991.

Ford, Henry. *The International Jew.* Appearing originally in the periodical published by the Ford Motor Co. in *The Dearborn Independent*, n.d.

Foster, Pat. *American Motors: The Last Independent.* Iola, Wisconsin: Krause Publications, 1993.

Gunnell, John. *Standard Catalogue of American Motors.* Iola, Wisconsin: Krause Publications, 1993.

Chevedden, John, & Kowalke, Ron. *Standard catalogue of Oldsmobile.* Iola, Wisconsin: Krause Publications, 1997.

Kowalke, Ron. *Standard Catalogue of Chevrolet.* Iola, Wisconsin: Krause Publications, 1998.

Sieber, Mary & Buttolph, Ken. *Standard Catalogue Of Cadillac.* Iola, Wisconsin: Krause Publications, 1995.

Kowalke, Ron. *Standard Catalogue of Independents.* Iola, Wisconsin: Krause Publications, 1999.

Periodicals

Collectible Automobile. Skokie, Illinois: Publications International. Various issues.

Special Interest Autos. Bennington, Vermont: Watering Inc. publishers. Various issues.

Cars & Parts. Sidney, Ohio: Amos Press, Inc. Various issues.